A HISTORY OF
AVIATION
IN ALDERNEY

A HISTORY OF AVIATION IN ALDERNEY

EDWARD PINNEGAR

AMBERLEY

First published 2010

Amberley Publishing Plc
Cirencester Road, Chalford,
Stroud, Gloucestershire, GL6 8PE

www.amberley-books.com

British Library Cataloguing in Publication Data.
A catalogue record for this book is available from the British Library.

ISBN 978 1 84868 981 7

Typeset in 10pt on 12pt Sabon.
Typesetting and Origination by Fonthill.
Printed in the UK.

Contents

Acknowledgements

I would like to thank Pete Andre, Sally Barber, Warwick Bayman, Bill Blanchard, Brian Bonnard, Ralph Burridge, Matt Capazario, Howard Chaloner, Doug Coxell, Neville Doyle, John Elsbury, Alexandra Gordon-Jones, Ian Haskell, Peter Hamer, Richard Hunt, Geoff Jones, Ron Kosys, Ian Larby, Malcolm Matthews, Don Oakden, Tim Osborne, Geoff Rennard, Matt Richmond, Peter Roberts, Bill Teasdale, Richard Vandervord, Keith Webster and Allan Wright for information and permission for the publication of photographs. Without the help and generosity of these people, the writing of this book would not have been possible. For this I am most sincerely grateful.

Thanks are also due to Aurigny Air Services and their *En Voyage* magazine team, and also to BN Historians (through Allan Wright) for their help and the many images offered for publication. Don Oakden and Alexandra Gordon-Jones were very forthcoming at the Alderney Museum, opening it outside of published hours, and were of great assistance with specialised and local knowledge.

Flight International Archives have also been of huge assistance with older plates. I should also like to thank my mother and father for their help and advice (with what might be seen to be a thankless task) and last, but most definitely not least, John Cox for his generous hospitality and also the many dinners he hosted!

Most importantly, however, I would like to thank my godfather, Tam Large, for inspiring me to write this book. As we were walking along the track that leads along the south of the airport, he asked me how long planes had been coming to Alderney. I told him what I knew about Aurigny, and he then asked me if anyone had ever written about the subject. When I told him that I was not aware of any such publications, he said, 'Why don't you have a go?' So I did.

For more information on the history of aviation in Alderney, please visit Warwick Bayman's website at www.alderneyaviationhistory.org.gg which documents the topic. It will be gradually built up and periodically updated.

Foreword

By Ian Larby

Honorary Secretary of Channel Islands Air Search

The 1930s saw immense growth in commercial aviation throughout Europe. The Channel Islands, whose only connection with the UK mainland was a notoriously rough sea crossing, were soon seen as an ideal destination for the fledgling airlines of that decade. The first commercial services had been operated in the 1920s by flying boats but these were irregular, being highly susceptible to sea conditions. The first regular land-based operations were focussed on Jersey, the largest island, where due to the lack of a suitable landing field, aircraft landed on a beach that was susceptible to the vagaries of the tide. The value of aviation was soon appreciated and there were moves to build aerodromes on all three islands. It was Alderney that had the distinction of being first to open a licensed aerodrome.

Since then, Alderney has been very dependent on air links for passenger traffic, perhaps to an even greater extent than Guernsey or Jersey, which have for many years been served by regular sea links.

Despite this very early start, no comprehensive history of aviation in Alderney has been written. Edward Pinnegar has set out to rectify this omission. He has undertaken a vast amount of research of the available information to produce this book. The advent of the internet has been valuable, but when sources are contradictory the accuracy of each one has to be questioned. The author has pursued this with patience, and the production of this book is a remarkable achievement. It is a valuable contribution to the history of aviation in the Islands.

It is a particularly fortunate coincidence that the seventy-fifth anniversary of Alderney Airport should fall in the same year as not only the fortieth anniversary of the Trislander but also the thirtieth anniversary of Channel Islands Air Search. The author's decision to mark this link, by donating part of the proceeds from sales of this book to Air Search, will help to ensure the continued success of this unique charity.

Introduction

For centuries, the only mode of transport to Alderney was by sea. The rough seas in the Channel Islands made it perilous for boats: numerous shipwrecks were recorded in the nineteenth century alone. When the era of aviation arrived, a land-based aerodrome was soon needed. In Guernsey, St Peter Port harbour had begun to accommodate seaplane operations while on Jersey, West Park (the stretch of beach between St Aubin and St Helier) was used by Jersey Airways with their de Havilland Dragons in the early 1930s.

In 1935, an enterprising Jerseyman named Captain Harold Benest MC, an affiliate of Jersey Airways, set up Alderney Development Ltd to build Alderney Airport and the Grand Hotel. He organised the acquisition of land (about 150 vergées from sixty mostly willing landowners, some owning very meagre amounts) on La Grande Blaye, in the southwest of the island, with the intention of turning it into an aerodrome.

All that was involved in building the airfield was the smoothing out of La Grande Blaye, re-sowing of the grass that covered it, and knocking down a few walls. Three runways were laid, all grass-surfaced, the main one being 500 yards long. The first airport building, consisting of a small, insalubrious, corrugated iron hut, was erected next to the main runway and the airport was declared ready for use in October 1935. There was a little trouble with outcrops of rock, but these were removed and the holes back-filled with soil. Two tractors were used to do the work, as well as manual workers.

The first officially recorded arrival at the new airport was a Channel Islands Airways Saro Windhover, which arrived on 15 August 1935. This marked the start of operations at the 'first' (see below) Channel Islands airport. The Alderney aerodrome licence was issued on 11 October 1935.

Although Alderney is generally regarded as having the first land-based aerodrome in the Channel Islands, this is a matter of debate. The claim was widely publicised by Jersey Airways at the time, but may just have been airline propaganda against a competitor, Cobham Air Routes. Construction had started on Alderney's aerodrome in April 1935, but in Guernsey, aircraft had been recorded flying in and out of L'Erée as early as September 1934 (although at that time L'Erée aerodrome was not licensed).

In November 1934, the Guernsey Aero Club had bought and transported an Avro Avian aircraft to Guernsey for training and touring purposes. However, those who argue that Alderney did have the first airport would say that it was at least the first licensed one and was the first in the Channel Islands to have scheduled flights.

Things have not changed all that much since then: in the autumn of 1935, services were being operated to Southampton and Guernsey, the first departure at 07.45 in the morning and the last flight returning at 18.15 – almost exactly the same timings as today's flights.

The airfield itself consisted of a hut, a grass strip and, not least, the controller, Miss Wilma Le Cocq (later Mrs Wilma Bragg). This remarkable lady came from a long-established Alderney family who had been on the island for many centuries. She apparently had more of a job herding farm animals off the air strip than dealing with the actual aircraft.

Wilma also had the job of coding and decoding telegraphs on the island and was, according to *Illustrated* magazine in 1939, the first and only female air traffic controller in the world at that time. A multitude of jobs was bestowed upon her, such as accounting, managing bookings and supervising the arrival and departure of aircraft.

The *Guernsey Evening Press* reported on 9 April 1936 that Miss Le Cocq, looking smart in her new uniform, was managing the aerodrome and running the office in St Anne. She drove the Customs officer out to the airport, completed all the paperwork next to the runway using the tractor top as a table, while at the same time keeping the passengers happy.

There were no telephones on the island so all bookings had to go by telegram at least two weeks in advance. Wilma's somewhat basic weather reports also had to go by telegram and her only helper was old Sam Allan, who acted as groundsman, loader, porter, fueller and operator of the aircraft starter batteries.

After the war, the airport building and garage were rebuilt, partly by German prisoners of war as well as British skilled labourers. The new buildings were staffed by six apparently underpaid firemen. Mains water was not installed until the present building was erected, although the airport gained mains electricity in 1954.

In 1962, to accommodate the new, larger Heron aircraft being operated increasingly by Jersey Airlines, the airport building was relocated a little to the north. Since then, the airport has had few upgrades, although there was one particular scheme undertaken between 1966 and 1967 when improvements were made which cost some £46,000 rather than the proposed £78,250. The authorities in Guernsey, who were responsible for the airport on Alderney, were well aware that the work done at this time had been little more than a stopgap measure and that Alderney's air communications were likely to remain a problem with airlines coming and going at a rate of knots.

The original recommendation was that Alderney should have a longer, paved runway. Since the army was prepared to construct the runway, the scheme would have cost only about £130,000. The States of Guernsey, however, turned down the project as being too ambitious. The improvements carried out were therefore a compromise.

In 1968, the asphalt runway was laid after much planning, costing £26,811 and measuring 880 metres (960 yards). This runway replaced one with a hoggin surface (a fine-grained hardcore) that had soon blown away and contaminated the water catchment near the airport. A hard runway was greatly needed because in 1960 alone, sixty-eight days had been lost to waterlogging. So, in the mid-1960s, the idea was put forward and accepted. However, there was debate as to the direction of the new runway

– one plan proposed a 7/25 alignment, which would have meant that it pointed further to the northeast, closer to the town – but the ultimately approved idea entailed a 9/27 runway, which due to magnetic changes is now the present 8/26 runway.

The new asphalt runway was extremely narrow in places, leaving it technically part grass, part tarmac. This was only resolved in 1989 when the runway was widened and partly resurfaced. In February 1986, the runway had been closed for the first time in twenty-five years due to waterlogging, which partly led to the final stage of widening in 1989. However, after this time, the grass space at the edge of the tarmac that had counted as part of the runway was no longer included, narrowing it from a total of 23 metres (12 metres of tarmac and 11 of grass) to just 18 metres.

The year 1988 saw the rebuilding of the control tower, turning it from an old wooden cabin into a new metal and glass structure. The control tower itself does not have radar and is quite basic even today with its telecommunications to Guernsey which also provides approach facilities for aircraft bound for Alderney. However, due to the size of the airport and the number of flights, the tower's facilities serve the airport more than adequately.

There also used to be a VOR radio navigational aid (a radio transmitter that pilots tune into so as to gauge their location in relation to it) to the south of the airport on the former site of the German Lager Sylt camp. This has now been replaced, albeit repositioned further to the east, with an NDB (a more basic, less accurate and cheaper navigational aid). The VOR had become unnecessary and expensive: a new VOR had recently been installed on Guernsey to coincide with the new airway (flight path) that overflew the island rather than the previous routing, which had passed over Alderney. Pilots heading to Alderney could use Guernsey's new VOR and then tune to the NDB when they came into close proximity to their destination. It had also cost the Civil Aviation Authority (CAA) a fortune due to it being one of the last in Britain to be permanently staffed by engineers – this was because it was extremely difficult to get them to the island when a fault developed.

Since then, there have been few upgrades to facilities, leaving the airport with the quaint feel that most in England lack, and passengers are not treated like animals as they are herded through what seem like endless security checks. It will hopefully be a long time, if ever, before Alderney reaches that stage.

While the author has attempted to provide a complete account of the history of aviation in Alderney, it is by no means exhaustive. Some have quipped that the island has had the largest number of airlines operate (and in some cases fail) in the smallest space over the years and it has therefore been somewhat difficult to record the full history. The author would therefore be grateful to receive any relevant information that has not been included in the present volume.

Chapter 1
1919-1939

The era of aviation began in Alderney in 1919 when two Avro 504L seaplanes were being flown to Jersey on 5 October. One aircraft reached its destination, but the other became disorientated in fog and had to land in the sea near Alderney. This resulted in its being wrecked on the Breakwater as it tried to enter Braye Bay.

The British Marine Navigation Company (BMNC) started operating from Southampton to Guernsey in September 1923, and on 13 October 1923 one of two Sea Eagle aircraft making the journey force-landed into rough seas near the Casquets. The other aircraft then landed in Braye harbour and pilot Henri Biard sounded the alarm.

The sea was incredibly rough, but Biard nevertheless took off again, damaging the floats and undersides of the boat as he was catapulted into the sky off a 40-foot roller, and got safely back to St Peter Port where he diverted a cargo boat to help. Fortunately, it was not needed as a Trinity House launch, *Lita*, had seen to the stricken aircraft whose crew, skipper Nick Allen and pilot Dave Ingrouille, had even managed to capsize their dinghy trying to get a tow rope across to the boat.

Luckily, the dinghy was finally secured and towed back to the shelter of Longis Bay. On 15 October, the stricken Sea Eagle flew to Guernsey for repairs, only to be sunk in St Peter Port harbour on 15 December 1926 after being accidentally rammed by another boat.

At this time in the early era of aviation, aircraft were not commonplace. It was therefore a very special event to see one overhead, especially on Alderney. There were no regular air services to the Channel Islands, and the only aircraft seen were not large and usually came from the south (the other Channel Islands and France), north (the United Kingdom) or east (also France). However, on the afternoon of 21 May 1927, an Alderney resident was playing sport on the Butes with a group of friends, when an aircraft was sighted coming from the west. This rather confused him as he had never seen an aircraft come from the west. It later turned out that this was Charles Lindbergh and his Ryan NYP *Spirit of St Louis*, performing the world's first non-stop transatlantic flight from New York to Paris. This amazing sight stayed with him for the rest of his life.

The first deliberate landing on the island was made on the shingle at Platte Saline beach at 9.00 a.m. on 4 August 1933. The aircraft, a Klemm L-25-1B monoplane from

Jersey carrying two joyriding passengers – a Mr Grayson and Mr Le Sueur who had each paid 2 shillings – landed and then had to be carried by a group of men from the stone crusher up onto the field above so that it could take off again from the road. The passengers stayed for a few days before making their own way back by sea.

However, there were soon calls for a land-based aerodrome: Captain Harold Benest MC therefore rented fields from landowners on La Grande Blaye in the southwest of the island. He did this from 1935 as part of his new company, Alderney Development Ltd, which also built the Grand Hotel. Here, with the help of Channel Islands Airways and its subsidiaries Jersey Airways and Guernsey Airways, Benest officially initiated the construction of the grass strip and Alderney's aerodrome on 1 April 1935, with Judge Mellish digging the first sod. As soon as the airfield was ready for use, the first flight arrived from Guernsey – a three-engined Saro Windhover amphibian owned by Guernsey Airways that landed on 22 May 1935.

Channel Islands Airways was investigating the viability of services to Alderney, so in 1934 their Saro Cloud (named *Cloud of Iona*) was dispatched to the island, full of States officials and island businessmen. It landed outside Braye and taxied in, before parking on the beach.

On 25 August 1934, however, Jersey Airways had an unfortunate incident on the beach at St Aubyn's in Jersey that was being used as the landing strip. It was a calm day, with little wind when, on his first day of flying with Jersey Airways as pilot of the de Havilland DH.84 Dragon aircraft, Geoffrey Wood took off in G-ACMO *St Ouen's Bay*. He had intended to become airborne between two groynes when his problems began; he said the following after the incident, in the next day's *Jersey Evening Post*:

> I taxied out on to the centre of the beach well clear of the wall. Soon after I had opened my throttles the aircraft started to swing to the right. I immediately applied full left rudder in order to check [compensate for] the swing, but the aircraft continued to swing to the right and I throttled back my port engine. She [the aircraft] still swung to the right and I saw that an accident was unavoidable. I then throttled back my other engine, stopping it, and pulled on the brakes. I was too late to avoid an accident.

Under normal circumstances, two boys playing near the groyne at that time would have been well away from any possible danger, but due to the swift and unexpected change of direction of the aircraft, one of the boys was directly in front of the aircraft. Striking the sea wall near the junction with the second groyne, none of the aircraft's occupants were injured but the boys, ten-year-olds Denis Dutot and Raymond Potigny, were struck by the wheels. Dutot was killed but Potigny survived his injuries; he recovered after a while in hospital.

In a similar incident a few days previously, a group of boys had been playing on the beach and onlookers had watched, horrified, convinced that the children were doomed. But they all scattered as the aircraft, a de Havilland DH.86 Express, flew a couple of feet above their heads. For one boy, though, it had been too late to move, but he sensibly remained calm and stayed still as the aircraft brushed his hair and the wheels passed either side of his shoulders. It was an accident waiting to happen.

Appearing to use him as the scapegoat, the Air Ministry at first blamed the pilot for his lack of experience, but this was later disproved. Although it was Geoffrey Wood's

A Klemm L-25 monoplane, the same type of aircraft that made the first deliberate landing on Alderney. Here, G-AAHW is pictured at Sywell, Northamptonshire. (*Mick Bajcar*)

Guernsey Airways' *Cloud of Iona*, a Saro A.19 Cloud aircraft, registered G-ABXW, sitting on Braye Beach in 1934 on a test flight. It crashed on 31 July 1936 between Guernsey and Jersey resulting in the tragic deaths of all seven occupants. (*Alderney Museum*)

first day of employment at Jersey Airways, he had carried out 2 hours and 40 minutes of flying at Heston airfield (an airfield at Hounslow, then acting as the main regional airport for London) four days previously.

This had been training for his new job at Jersey Airways and he had been required to do landing tests in the DH.86 to endorse his licence on this aircraft. He had 690 hours of previous flying experience with the RAF (all with single-engined aircraft, admittedly).

The *Jersey Evening Post* carried the headline 'J'ACCUSE' in its Monday issue and blamed the island authorities, while at the same time calling for an immediate and thorough enquiry. At this time, Jersey Airways operated services to Paris, Alderney, Southampton, Portsmouth and Heston, together with a short-lived service to Rennes.

By October 1935, Alderney's land-based aerodrome was very nearly ready for use. There was a need for additional drainage and also a little more re-seeding, but no major work remained to be done. Two tractors were working to prepare the airfield and these, along with a group of manual labourers, helped to remove rocky outcrops that were posing a problem on the Grande Blaye. However, the Channel Islands Airways' Saro Windhover was still out of action and the airline had yet to make request stops available on services from Jersey to the mainland.

Arrangements were made in early March 1936 for Miss Wilma Le Cocq (later Mrs Wilma Bragg) to visit Jersey for training as Jersey Airways' representative on the island. According to residents, she was quite an attractive young lady from a well-known local family, with blonde hair and blue eyes. She was to run the airport and office until the war.

The day of 27 March saw the first request stop on Alderney, which was made by a DH.86 from Jersey bound for Heston. It landed two passengers, a Mr Gordon Rice and a Mrs Faul. They both returned to Jersey the next day, taking 'Bill' Caldwell, who had flown in from Southampton, with them. (Caldwell was described by others as a 'dour Scot' who was a pilot himself and had previously owned Scottish Motor Traction.) As Mr Rice was a solicitor, it is thought that the reason they visited was a legal matter.

One highly memorable moment for passengers occurred on 31 March 1936, when those on afternoon flights in the Channel Islands had fantastic views of the airship *Hindenburg* heading west en route across the Atlantic. The airship was sighted ten miles south of Alderney by a Jersey Airways aircraft at 5.10 p.m. and passengers were close enough to see the airship's registration number: LZ129.

However, a week later on 6 April, a group of Channel Island passengers had a far less pleasant experience when their aircraft was struck by lightning, rendering the radio and compass useless and tearing fabric all over the plane. Luckily nobody was injured, although the idea of being encased in a small tube along with several gallons of aviation fuel was not a pleasant one.

The much heralded Southampton–Alderney–Guernsey service was finally launched by Channel Islands Airways on 6 April 1936 with a daily service except on Wednesdays. De Havilland DH.89 Rapides were used between Southampton and Alderney, and passengers were then transferred to the Windhover amphibian aircraft for the Alderney–Guernsey leg. St Peter Port harbour was Guernsey Airways' terminus as Cobham Air Routes had the monopoly on the land aerodrome at L'Erée.

Piloting the Windhover was Bill Halmshaw, an experienced flying boat pilot who had studied law at Sheffield University but, finding it unexciting, had joined the RAF at the age of twenty-three. He trained at Sealand (an RAF base in Wales, operational from 1916 to 2004) and then spent five years flying with 201 and 210 flying boat squadrons, before being transferred to the Reserve in 1936. He joined Jersey Airways immediately afterwards.

The first leg, from Guernsey to Alderney, took 33 minutes against a 40 mph head-wind and the passengers were Mr Kane, a reporter from the *Guernsey Star*, as well as a Mr Pritchard. Two young brothers (aged five and six respectively) also travelled, named Peter and John Newton. Mr Pritchard returned to Guernsey in the amphibian while Mr Kane and the Newtons carried on to Southampton in the DH.89, becoming the first passengers to do so in that direction. They crossed the Channel at 6000 feet and the pilot Douglas Brecknell (Jersey Airways' youngest pilot and brother of Guernsey Airways pilot, Adrian Brecknell), circled the King George dock in order to get a better view of the splendid *Queen Mary*.

The Windhover amphibian was regularly grounded due to technical problems. On several occasions, engine problems kept the aircraft from flying. On another occasion, the undercarriage lowered itself while the aircraft was taxiing on the sea near Jersey with the result that the flying boat was stranded.

In addition to these problems, it was also a notoriously uncomfortable aircraft. The air correspondent at the *Guernsey Star* described it as a 'veritable hen-coop with wings ... you can't move a limb and you sit in an atmosphere of petrol fumes with the mechanic continually climbing over your knees ... taking off the sea, you spend most of your time ineffectively trying to keep dry. Water literally pours in from the supposedly closed windows.' Public opinion of the aircraft was therefore not high.

Alderney airport was definitely still new to Channel Islands Airways pilots – and it showed on 29 June 1936 when a de Havilland DH.84 Dragon overran the runway. The aircraft, piloted by a Mr Martin, was laden with six passengers. Unfortunately, the pilot was a little too fast and the aircraft ran out of airfield, striking a bank, breaking the starboard propeller and damaging the undercarriage.

Mr Martin was quite a new face in Guernsey Airways, having only flown with them for a couple of months. He claimed, after the crash, that his brakes had failed. Whether this was true or not was never ascertained. (It is said that after an incident, the insurer blames pilot error, the pilot blames design error, and the designer blames the pilot for trusting the aircraft.) But Dragon brakes were notoriously unreliable. Martin also said that he had been given the choice of careering into the earth bank or hitting a herd of six cows – and, being an animal lover at heart, he chose the former.

A passenger, Mr Head, had left Beckenham that morning with a Miss V. Edwards and then caught a train from Waterloo at 8.30 a.m. for Eastleigh, where they had boarded the aircraft. Mr Head commented after the incident that the pilot had seemed to have a problem positioning the aircraft for approach, and had circled the airfield twice before landing. Visibility was bad and there had been lousy weather throughout that June. When the pilot did bring the aircraft down, Head stated that it was a perfect landing until the aircraft overran.

By 1937, Jersey Airways had started a service from Jersey to Brighton (Shoreham) and this was proving successful, along with their already established services from Jersey to Exeter, Southampton, Alderney and Heston. All of the services from Guernsey and Jersey to the south and southeast of England had to operate over Alderney, because of a prohibited area over the Cap de la Hague and the Cherbourg Peninsula. There is, as it happens, a prohibited area over the same site today, as well as one over Flamanville (further down the coast), both due to the location of nuclear facilities.

Wilma Le Cocq was becoming ever busier as the aviation business grew, and such were her charms that there was an ever growing waiting list for those who wished to take over the job of her assistant, the elderly Sam Allen.

On Friday 4 November 1938, a disaster struck Jersey Airways. There was a south-westerly wind blowing 15 mph, and a completely overcast cloud layer at 120 feet that had been fog earlier in the day. It had been just another normal day at the airport at St Peter on Jersey, and the de Havilland DH.86 Express, G-ACZN *St Catherine's Bay* took off for Southampton at 10.52 a.m.

The pilot, A. G. M. (Geoff) Cary, an ex-RAF officer, had joined the airline the previous winter after spending time in India. His radio operator was Jack Lyons, an ex-merchant navy 'A' licence holder. They took off into the cloud and transmitted a normal radio message saying that they were climbing in cloud through 300 feet.

However, the DH.86 suddenly emerged from the cloud in the direction of St Peter and dived towards St Peter's Farm and a narrow lane. It continued to plummet and hit a field named 'La Bataille' near the lane, before bouncing through a hedge and smashing into a bank on the other side of the lane. It exploded, with a jet of flame 50 feet high and 30 feet wide, and the contents of the aircraft were hurled within 100 square yards of the burning wreckage, which included bodies, books, suitcases and a teddy bear. All

A Miles M.57 Aerovan of Pickford Aviation at Guernsey Airport in the late 1930s. (*Collection Charlie Verrall*)

fourteen occupants died in an appalling air disaster that was to be the bloodiest day for Channel Islands aviation for many years to come.

The Air Ministry described this tragic accident as an error of airmanship due to the climb turning into a left-hand sideslip – the pilot accidentally turning the aircraft at an altitude where it is still too low for him to be able to recover control. The *Jersey Evening Post* described the tragic event as the 'blackest day in the history of Jersey aviation'.

After the investigation, the airline began to recover and get back to business as usual. Of course, in such a small island community, such an air disaster and the associated loss of life is a huge blow to the entire population, especially with well-known islanders among the dead. This also tarnished the airline's reputation and also gave air travel as a whole a bad reputation in the Channel Islands.

Jersey Airways continued to operate until the German occupation in mid-1940, during which time aircraft were hidden in the same way that those in Guernsey had been. Guernsey Aero Club hid their Avro Avian in a shed at L'Erée, from where, prior to the opening of the new airport, they were still flying.

On 5 May 1939, the new Guernsey airport opened at La Villiaze, a site that had been selected by the States on 30 October 1935 as being suitable. However, as its opening was little more than a year before the occupation, scheduled air services did not have the opportunity to flourish, although there were short-lived services to Southampton, Heston, Brighton and Exeter.

Another operator to service Alderney on an irregular basis before the war was Pickford Aviation. Run by 'Pick' Pickford, it operated Miles M.57 Aerovans on charter services to Alderney until the Nazi occupation brought this to an end.

Chapter 2
1940-1945

After war had been declared, Jersey Airways was forced to implement price rises throughout its international network. Inter-island flights remained at fifteen shillings. Flights became increasingly irregular with Jersey Airways continuing to fly the routes from the island to Dinard and Southampton–Heston. Passengers destined for Exeter and Brighton were left to make their own arrangements to get home.

Guernsey Airways also operated to Alderney on a Southampton–Alderney–Guernsey rotation with de Havilland DH.89 Dragon Rapides and DH.86 Expresses. It operated in conjunction with Jersey Airways and operated from Guernsey to London.

The company officially operated from 1934 to 1945 (but did not fly during the occupation) and suffered one accident where a Saro A.19 Cloud aircraft (registered G-ABXW and named *Cloud of Iona*) crashed into the sea on a flight from Guernsey to Jersey on 31 July 1936. The aircraft had to land in the sea on a stormy evening due to loss of engine power and all seven souls onboard were drowned.

This served as a huge blow to Channel Islands Airways, both to their reputation and their finances. Guernsey Airways did not operate in 1937, leading to a loss of £2,069. Claims and expenses from the loss of *Cloud of Iona* amounted to £736, while depreciation, insurance and other charges related to the Windhover accounted for the princely sum of £829. The airline also had to prepare to pay out more in claims to a chronically asthmatic man who lost his wife in the accident.

But something far more important was hanging over islanders – the war was looming. When at last it was clear that the Germans were going to take the Channel Islands, Alderney was evacuated. Nevertheless, the departing islanders still had time to block the grass runway with a few lorries and heavy vehicles.

The island was invaded by German forces on 2 July 1940. Early that day, a large troop-carrying aircraft had to fly back to Guernsey because of the obstructed runway. Although it was unable to land, a two-seat Fieseler Storch, an aircraft that could be put down using less than 100 feet of unprepared space, was able to touch down. Two such aircraft landed on La Grande Blaye, and their crews set about clearing the lorries and various obstructions before the larger aircraft could bring the bulk of the occupying force.

The German occupying forces were somewhat cautious as to whether and when a British counterattack would take place. So, in early August 1940, a group of Luftwaffe plane spotters were sent to the island. The group of twelve arrived on 2 or 3 August with a corporal on a Junkers Ju 52 transport aircraft, which had flown via Dinard and Querqueville (an airfield that no longer exists, located to the west of Cherbourg). Later, to deter parachutists, they drove steel spikes into the ground as well as ploughing huge furrows across the runways to stop aircraft landing.

But Alderney did not go entirely untouched by the Allies during the Second World War. J. W. Merriam, a pilot for the Special Operations Executive (SOE), apparently flew into Alderney on 19 November 1942; this was reported by someone else on his behalf for the BBC feature *People's War*.

Reportedly, he was summoned to the airfield at Christchurch, Hampshire and instructed to fly a Westland Lysander aircraft to Alderney and land it on Braye beach. The reason for this extraordinary expedition was that a French fisherman, working in a resistance group, had had his vessel taken by the Germans from Braye beach. He was therefore unable to escape the island.

Merriam was briefed that the fisherman would be wearing a white hat so he could be easily seen by the pilot, but the man was therefore not easily distinguishable from

The airfield after the occupying forces had ploughed trenches through it to make the landing of enemy aircraft almost impossible. It is seen here in an aerial photograph taken on a reconnaissance mission. (*Brian Bonnard*)

Photographs taken by reconnaissance aircraft during the Second World War of Alderney in occupied hands. The picture on the left shows the Braye and Crabby area of the island while the picture on the right shows Longis and the Quesnard area. (*Alderney Museum*)

the abundant seabirds. He was to touch down only once, so there would be no second chances. Sure enough, he touched down and the fisherman was still climbing up the ladder as Merriam opened the throttles and took off again.

This account is disputed by some because it is unlikely that he would have been able to fly an aircraft in without considerable resistance from the many anti-aircraft guns on the island. Therefore, the only plausible explanation is that, to reduce the noise, Merriam had climbed to a high altitude over the Channel, idled his engine, and then descended onto the island.

The Germans also built a concentration camp named Lager Sylt to the south of the airfield, one of four camps (the only concentration camp – the others were labour camps) on the island and the only four on British soil.

The prime minister Winston Churchill also sent reconnaissance aircraft during the war, which returned with several pictures of the Channel Islands. He deemed a full-scale attack on the islands risky, (although there were some smaller operations), so the Germans were able to stay there, strengthening their Atlantic Wall, until the tide of the war turned in the Allies favour.

On 2 and 8 November 1941, two Supermarine Spitfires crashed on Alderney in unrelated incidents. These were the only air crashes on the island during the war so it is a coincidence that they both occurred within a week of each other. These crashes, as well as some other wartime crashes near the island, are chronicled in Chapter 7 in greater detail.

Chapter 3
1946-1967

Alderney was restored to Channel Islands Airways' timetable on 1 February 1946. The company had restarted operations after the war with six former RAF de Havilland DH.89 Rapides and the airport was high on the list of States' priorities. The first flight arrived from Liverpool – a chartered DH.89 Rapide carrying Bert Hammond and his father (from the Campania Inn), the island having been mostly de-mined and re-inhabited after the homecoming. British European Airways, the new state-owned British airline, started flying scheduled services to Alderney after toppling Channel Islands Airways.

At this time, the British government had announced the nationalisation of most British transport services: the four main railway lines, the bus services and most airlines were all included. Although it seemed obvious that Channel Islands Airways would be nationalised, there was a large and fierce local opposition to the scheme. Plans were hatched to sell shares throughout the Channel Islands and/or have Channel Islands directors on the boards, but these came to nothing when the UK government quashed the uprising by threatening to prevent the airline from using mainland airports.

Sadly, on 31 March 1947, Channel Islands Airways ceased to exist. This caused huge resentment throughout the Islands, making residents feel discriminated against by the mainland government. Now there was only a large impersonal airline flying into the Islands called British European Airways. This major change meant the start of a new period of aviation history in Alderney.

It marked the sad end to the era of early aviation in the Channel Islands. British European Airways, or BEA as it was known, started services to Guernsey and Jersey as well as some mainland airports. In addition, they also pioneered post-war services to what today is one of the UK's busiest airports and indeed still is the busiest airport with a single operational runway in the world: Gatwick. No other airline was allowed to operate services that competed directly with them, which led to quite a limited service.

Wilma Le Cocq did not return to her post at the airport after the war and was replaced by the young Maurice Rick. He had been a fitter at the RAF maintenance unit at Feltwell and had come to Alderney just before the war to mend a Handley Page Harrow bomber that had performed an emergency landing on 6 April 1939, bouncing

The Channel Islands Airways terminal building at Alderney, seen here in 1947, newly built with the help of German POWs. However, the company as a private entity ceased to exist on 31 March 1947, when it was nationalised. (*Alderney Museum*)

over a hedge onto the airfield. He stayed throughout August of that year to complete the job, leaving the island just before the war, returning after it to fill the post.

Also after the war, the airport building and garage were rebuilt by German prisoners of war and some British skilled labourers, and was staffed by six apparently underpaid firemen. Mains water was not installed until the present building was erected in 1968, although the airport gained mains electricity in 1954.

Another initiative after the war was the Market Gardens Scheme, which ran from the winter of 1945. This scheme's aim was to turn the island into a communal farm and business during the first few years after the war (with adults earning £3 a week, a good wage for many an islander), but later to export the products cultivated.

One plant grown under the scheme was daffodils. The cultivation started off quite meagrely, but by the mid-1950s, five million were being exported each year. Alderney's entire population of around 1,500 struggled to pick all these flowers, and professional pickers and manual labourers had to be flown in on special charters from Lincolnshire.

The year 1948 saw Alderney hand over most of its administration to Guernsey. This included the airport, which is still overseen by the Public Services Department whose chief politician still holds the airfield license. The airport director in Guernsey (Colin Le Ray at time of writing) also oversees the operations in Alderney.

The early 1950s saw a trial service to Alderney from an airport known today as a major hub, which probably would not exist if the service had not been pioneered. The

British European Airways' de Havilland DH.89 Rapides serviced Alderney from the other Channel Islands and also from Gatwick, the airport's first scheduled service after the Second World War. (*Ian Larby*)

airport is now thought of as an international hub with flights to sun-soaked destinations all over the world. However, what is not generally recognised was that the first regular scheduled destination from Gatwick after the Second World War was, in fact, Alderney. BEA ran the trial from 1950 to 1952 on a summer-only basis, employing de Havilland DH.89 Dragon Rapides on the service.

Gatwick's future had been in jeopardy after the RAF relinquished control of the airfield after the war. It had been used as an airfield since the 1920s, with a few scheduled services by pre-war independent airlines such as British Airways (a different airline from that which we know today). In effect, therefore, Alderney saved the airfield from closure as it would have been shut after the war had there not been a very good reason to keep it open. At this stage, the former racecourse was little more than a grass strip, although BEA in conjunction with the British government soon decided it would be convenient as the 'other' London airport, an alternative to Heathrow.

The first flight to Alderney was flown by G-AHXZ, (G- being the prefix for all British aircraft registrations and the rest of the letters identifying each individual aircraft). The service proved to be a great success, and it eventually led to BEA's Channel Islands flights being transferred from Heathrow and being flown from the newly built Gatwick along with a multitude of other services – all thanks to Alderney's role as the guinea pig.

A new arrival in 1952 was that of Birkett Air Services, which operated a Croydon–Alderney route using DH.89 Rapides. This service was however short-lived with the airline pulling out shortly afterwards.

The main runway at Alderney was extended by 170 feet in 1953 to allow the de Havilland Heron to fly in. The airlines using the island had previously employed de Havilland Rapides, Dragons or Expresses, but gradually more capacity was required, necessitating larger aircraft.

On Friday 16 October 1956, the prototype Handley Page Herald visited the Channel Islands. It made a short visit to Alderney, taking off in less than half of the 950-yard grass runway that was available, and landing in only 700 yards. It is, at time of writing, still the largest aircraft to have landed on the island.

This was very impressive and a good selling point for the Herald, leading to Jersey Airlines buying three of the aircraft. It was relatively quiet, efficient and attractive for

The Handley Page Herald taking off in 1956 in less than half of the 950-yard strip available to it at Alderney. (*Ralph Burridge*)

The Herald pictured behind employees from Handley Page as well as officials from the States of Alderney. Tommy Rose was also present. (*By kind permission of Flight International*)

passengers and airlines alike and was therefore highly popular. It also had good leg and head room, so much so that a man 6 feet tall could stand up straight in the cabin.

While it would be fair to say the Herald is the largest aircraft to have visited the island, it should also be noted that the airfield has also welcomed Douglas DC3 Dakotas – two flew in during the summer of 1979, one on a proving flight for its operator and the other carrying parts for Alderney's VOR and DME navigational equipment. Behind the Dakota in terms of size, the island has also seen a 748 Andover (an RAF variant of the Hawker Siddeley 748 medium-sized turboprop) of the Royal Flight, which carried members of the royal family. A more regular arrival that usually visits annually is a Cessna Citation business jet, operated from a private grass strip in Scandinavia – no mean feat for a comparatively heavy jet aircraft.

Among those present at the Herald's visit were Sydney Herivel, President of Alderney at the time, and Tommy Rose (1895-1968), aviation pioneer and Alderney resident. Rose had immigrated to Alderney from England but was soon well settled into island life, taking on the Marais Hotel and later the Grand Hotel on the Butes, which was sadly gutted by fire in 1981. He did not run the Marais Hotel as a normal sort of guesthouse, as Elizabeth McNamer who waitressed there recalled. She once served an extremely rich man who grew up in Essex Castle and was educated at Eton and Oxford – indeed, he told her he was so rich that he owned a private army in Arabia (even if he was short, bald, and only thirty-five).

Additionally, a Russian prince named Alexis had stayed and invited her to Sark on his yacht. He had visited this island at the same time as a nostalgic German soldier

"Engine still running perfectly after 25,000 miles without any attention"

says TOMMY ROSE of the
GIPSY-SIX
ENGINE IN HIS MILES FALCON

Tommy Rose (1895-1968), aviation pioneer and Alderney resident, featured in an advertisement for Gipsy-Six aero engines. (*Alderney Museum*)

who had been posted there during the war and who remarked to Elizabeth, 'It's good to be back!' which left her somewhat puzzled considering the goings on during the occupation.

Tommy Rose, though, had most notably flown from London to Cape Town in 1936 – a record-breaking flight of just 3 days, 17 hours and 38 minutes, arriving at Wingfield Aerodrome in Cape Town on 9 February 1936.

The flight was undertaken in a Miles M3B Falcon six aircraft, which was later the centre of a debate sparked by an article in the *Daily Telegraph* in November 1984. The paper had reported that the curator of Alderney Museum was having problems tracking down the colour of the aircraft; this led to his receiving more than twenty letters, many of which conflicted with each other as some said that it was green and yellow while others said it was a light brown.

Although there were photographs of the aircraft after the flight, these were in black and white, which meant that identifying colours was made a good deal more difficult. George H. Miles, the brother of the founder of the former aircraft manufacturer, later confirmed that the aircraft was cream with red registration lettering (as had been reported in a few of the letters); he stated in the correspondence that: 'the actual shade of cream was pale (approximately the same as Jersey milk) and the red was scarlet.'

In another response to the article, Harold Best-Devereux, an avid light aviation enthusiast and once chairman of the Popular Flying Association, wrote in a letter in 1984: 'Tommy was a wonderful figure in aviation. He had a great liver and he was a great liver – he needed it to cope with all the booze he could put away...' This, from what can be ascertained from those who knew him, could be seen as quite an accurate representation of his character.

Rose had been much involved with aviation during the Great War. While flying on the Western Front, he scored nine victories and later won the Distinguished Flying Cross. Later, in 1932, he set up the second regular air service to the Isle of Man called the Isle of Man Air Service, operating from Liverpool (Speke). He had acquired the prototype Cutty Sark aircraft (registered G-AAIP) for the air service, which was the first aircraft made by Saunders Roe Ltd, an aircraft manufacturer that was active for a large chunk of the early twentieth century.

In 1935, he had won the King's Cup race with an average speed of 176 mph. During the war, he had developed his own extremely skilled flying. Once, he had been approaching his base aerodrome when a blackbird flew in front of him. Rose made a skilful sideslip and looked on as German gunfire peppered his previous position. He later said that if he had not seen the blackbird (which he was unfortunately unable to avoid) he would have been shot down and would probably have lost his life.

Back in Alderney, BEA were having problems. In 1956, they withdrew all capacity from the airport. Fortunately, Jersey Airlines came to the rescue and stood in to fill the gap. The year 1957 saw de Havilland Herons replace the de Havilland Rapides completely, and these provided a twice-daily service until BUIA (see below) pulled out in 1969.

In the 1950s, the British government relaxed its tight grip on the British airline industry, allowing other privately owned airlines to operate for the first time in twenty-five years. Silver City operated to Alderney for a while from Southampton, and in February 1959

The Alderney airport buildings covered in snow after a blizzard in the 'big freeze' of winter 1963. (*Alderney Museum*)

East Anglian Flying Services (trading as Channel Airways) filed for permission to run an Ipswich–Southend–Rochester–Shoreham–Alderney–Guernsey–Jersey service. This went ahead, but only included Alderney for a short time, later flying straight on to Guernsey, utilising a de Havilland Dove.

In 1962, it was decided by all parties that for the operation of Herons, the terminal building was too close to the runway. It was therefore relocated a little to the north. During the winter of 1963, the island had its coldest winter for many years: everything, including the airport, was completely covered in snow.

One of BEA's Sikorsky S.61 helicopters paid several visits to Alderney in 1964, the first aircraft from the airline to visit the island since it pulled out in 1956. The 28-seat helicopter was used on the Penzance–Isles of Scilly service but frequented the Channel Islands during the mid-1960s when the runway at Jersey airport was being resurfaced. This operation could only be carried out during daylight hours and took place between 9.00 a.m. and 5.00 p.m., from November to February.

BEA's Station Superintendant, Eddie West, thought that the midday link with London should continue and considered the S.61 to be perfect. During its service in the Channel Islands, it flew 4,306 passengers between Guernsey and Jersey and would make multiple trips during the Christmas period.

As well as visiting Alderney a few times, the helicopter made one visit to Sark on a Sunday during Easter 1966. Given that the island does not allow motor traffic or aeroplanes, the Dame of Sark had to grant special permission for an ill resident needing treatment at the Princess Elizabeth Hospital in Guernsey to get there because the ambulance launch boat was unavailable.

The Sark fire brigade were on standby as the helicopter took off with BEA officials, the patient and some first aiders onboard. The field had recently been used by grazing cows, and subsequently its use as a makeshift helipad was questioned by the fire brigade – as the helicopter took off, so did a number of cow pats!

In 1966 and 1967, improvements were made at the airport costing £46,000. Only half of the work that would have solved the many problems was carried out resulting in it being only a temporary measure. This was partly due to the reluctance of the States of Guernsey who deemed it too risky an investment and would not spend the money, even though the army had offered to do the work at a reduced price.

While the improvements were being made, Jersey Airlines was acquired by British United Airways (BUA), to form British United (CI) Airways, which in turn later formed British United Island Airways (BUIA).

In 1968, the part-asphalt runway was laid – costing £26,811 – and was marginally longer than its predecessor, measuring 880 metres rather than the previous 860 metres

A British United Island Airways de Havilland Heron seen here at London Gatwick Airport. (*Alex Christie*)

(950 yards). As well as this, a new air traffic control tower was built and a larger terminal was also constructed. The new runway replaced one with a hoggin surface (a fine-grained hardcore), which had soon blown away and contaminated the water catchment near the airport. The runway was regarded as a great asset, for in 1960 alone sixty-eight days were lost because of the waterlogging of the grass runways. During the renovations of 1967-1968 a temporary air service ran to the island using Cessna 337s.

Chapter 4
1968-1980

The next decade proved to be somewhat turbulent. BUIA had agreed to supply the additional services that the people of Alderney wanted, providing nearly 2,000 extra seats from England between April and October – mainly concentrated on Southampton, as the islanders had requested. In return, BUIA wished to increase prices so that Gatwick–Alderney would cost £6; Southampton–Alderney £5; and Guernsey–Alderney £2. The fares structure before the price increases had been: Gatwick–Alderney weekdays, £4 9s; Fridays and Sundays, £5 8s; and on Saturdays, £6 11s.

However, in 1967, BUIA unfortunately ran into trouble when it disclosed that its Alderney services were losing £40,000 per year, and had been a 'dead weight' operation for some time. Even after a considerable amount of lobbying from States members and residents to keep the air routes, the airline cut the inter-island routes and only ran Alderney–Southampton. The rises in fares had left them quite unpopular.

Morton Air Services, their subsidiary (related to former Alderney States member Fred Morton), filled the gap temporarily. They only operated 'on behalf of' BUIA and therefore the States had to act quickly; now that they only had a stand-in operator, the permanency of the 'lifeline' air link had been lost. As a possible solution to the problem, they headhunted Sir Derrick Bailey – who had recently started GlosAir of Staverton, Gloucestershire, a company which had recently taken delivery of a new Britten-Norman Islander – to start a profitable airline to serve Alderney. And he did.

On 1 March 1968, GlosAir performed its first flight from Alderney to Guernsey using its only aircraft, the Britten-Norman Islander. The now ubiquitous Islander had nine seats and cost little to operate compared to other aircraft of that size in its day. Later, in 1968, Bailey moved the entire GlosAir operation from the UK to Alderney, and finally Aurigny Air Services was born.

On 1 April 1969, the thirty-fourth anniversary of the beginning of construction of the Alderney airfield, air traffic control was introduced. This followed an incident the year before in which a de Havilland Heron took off from the wrong end of the runway, therefore not facing into the wind, which in turn would mean it would have less lift – this could have presented unforeseen dangers to the aircraft.

BUIA left Alderney completely with one week's notice that year, and Aurigny took over their last remaining Alderney–Southampton route. Before long, Aurigny was beginning

GlosAir's Islander, G-AVCN, also one of the first Britten-Norman Islanders, can be distinguished from early Aurigny colours by the logo on the tail plane: early Aurigny aircraft displayed a lion (the Alderney crest) while GlosAir had just the stripe with a small circular symbol.
(*BN Historians through Allan Wright*)

to flourish and by 1970 it was operating from Alderney to Southampton, Guernsey and Jersey, and from Jersey to the French airfield at Granville (although this route was short-lived), as well as from Cherbourg to Southampton. By now the company had eight Islanders, nineteen pilots and over fifty ground and handling staff.

The Channel Islands' new airline was on a roll. Incredibly, the business was profitable even at such an early stage in the airline's history, and it was showing a fast rate of growth – which is no mean feat for a small carrier new to the market. This seemed almost impossible given how much British United Airways and its predecessors had complained about the lack of profitability, possibility and potential in the Channel Islands.

Aurigny has always been an airline committed to innovation, and in 1971 it introduced the Islander's big sister to its fleet, the Britten-Norman Trislander. The Trislander was a rather mad idea, taking its inspiration from airliners with three jets, such as the McDonnell Douglas DC10 and Lockheed L-1011 Tristar. (In fact, in its early operational days, it was frequently referred to as the 'Clockwork Tristar'.) Amazingly, the development from stretched Islander to Trislander took just eight weeks.

Britten-Norman was soon offering the Trislander with an auxiliary 350 lb (1.56 kN or 158 kg) rocket to provide extra thrust on takeoff. Aurigny never took advantage of this, but some pilots would argue that the Trislander could do with a little more power. Indeed, in the 1980s, one owned by another airline was flying so slowly over the English Channel that it was asked quite seriously by a Brussels air traffic controller what type of helicopter it was that appeared as BN2 on his screens (this being the Trislander designation code).

On the same day as its maiden flight, 11 September 1970, it flew straight up to the Farnborough Airshow as a surprise static exhibit. Most aircraft undergo numerous test flights before even considering entering an airshow so this was definitely a one-off.

There had been a rumour of a stretched Islander, but nobody expected this. Crowds looked on in amazement as this novel piece of engineering taxied to its parking area. In the opinion of most, the aircraft looked like a concept that should never have got further than the drawing board. Popular opinion was that the third engine should have been placed on the nose and, in any case, the tail fin looked lopsided. Although not the most graceful thing with wings, the Trislander was to be a highly successful aircraft in the years to come.

The Trislander was not Britten-Norman's only slightly mad idea. There had also been plans for a Weekender – a biplane which could be folded up and put in a box in minutes, which would be ideal for use at weekends. Another project was a 100-seater STOL aircraft named the Mainlander, which could either adopt a cargo configuration or seat 100 passengers. Intended especially for third world countries, the aircraft would

The prototype Trislander, taxiing on a wet afternoon at the Farnborough Airshow on Monday 11 September 1970, having just completed one of its first flights (the very first one being a test flight that morning). Note the lack of an upper tail section. (*Alex Christie*)

comfortably land on a 500 m (1,700 ft) unprepared grass strip. Although both of these ideas came to nothing, they still got as far as the drawing board.

Aurigny was the first airline in the world to use the Trislander and is to this day the type's largest operator. the aircraft had eighteen seats (including the two pilots' seats), and three Lycoming piston engines that were jovially reputed to make the regular traveller stone deaf in five years.

One former pilot on Alderney told the author of an audiologist based in the East Midlands whose 'party trick' was being able to tell what type of aircraft a pilot had flown regularly by which pitch in their hearing was impaired. He was correct about seventy per cent of the time, but the only aircraft he was always right about were those designed by Britten-Norman.

Two years after Aurigny's formation in 1970, Westward Airways, an airline that operated Britten-Norman Islanders in the southwest of England, the Scillies, and also between Gatwick and Heathrow, applied to fly from Gatwick to Sandown (Isle of Wight) to Alderney, and also Newquay–Plymouth–Alderney–Guernsey–Jersey. Both BUIA and Aurigny opposed the application and the licence was not granted.

In 1972, Aurigny's Islanders were flying parts for Concorde from Cherbourg to Southampton, and the following year Trislanders were put full-time on the Alderney–

A Westward Airways Britten-Norman Islander, seen here at Gatwick Airport. The airline had applied to fly to Alderney but the license was not granted due to strong opposition. (*Caz Caswell, AirTeamImages*)

Southampton route. In 1974, a flight from Alderney to Cherbourg would have cost you just £17.30. Soon after, in 1975, Aurigny carried its 1,000,000th passenger, a Mr Malcolm Gulliver.

Also in the early 1970s, Peter Moss, an Alderney builder and entrepreneur hosted the first so-called International Air Rally. This was largely a success and he hosted it for the next few years. It was dropped by the mid-1970s though, and only after about a decade's gap in 1985 did the International Air Rally resume as the Alderney Fly-In (as part of the 50th anniversary celebrations of the airport), which was so popular that it became an annual fixture the following year.

This, along with the Alderney Air Races, was now one of the most important events in Alderney's aviation calendar. The largest fly-in, in 1994, boasted 152 aircraft. Fitting them into such a small airfield proved quite a challenge. Every available space was used, with aircraft parked not only on the old helipad, but on additional purpose-made grass parking areas around the airfield, as well as the triangular area south of the airfield, formed by the intersection of all three runways.

Because Concorde had started crossing the Atlantic on supersonic scheduled services in 1976, a sonic-boom was soon rattling across the sea towards the West Country and Alderney as the aircraft broke the sound barrier. This nuisance was solved in 1977,

Alderney Airport looking more like London Heathrow: the Alderney Fly-In was at one time very popular – at its climax in 1994, over 150 aircraft visited the island for one of the most important aviation events of the year. (*Ralph Burridge*)

when an Alderney resident (though it is unclear who it was) came up with a new flight path for Air France Concordes which involved a short cut. This meant that less fuel was required so two extra passengers could be carried on the Paris–Washington service (only outbound, though, as inbound the aircraft were at this point descending), and the sonic-boom would no longer be heard. However, the sonic-boom could now be heard in Guernsey instead, and according to a Guernsey resident some people would check their clocks when they heard the rumble at precisely 4.05 p.m.

There was to be another 'first' for Aurigny, the airline that had saved Alderney's lifeline air links. It became the first airline in the world to ban smoking in its aircraft. Now phasing out the Islander and receiving increasing numbers of Trislanders from Britten-Norman on the Isle of Wight, it also operated from Guernsey to Cherbourg.

One of the advantages (or possibly disadvantages) of the new French service was the huge demand in the Channel Islands for fine food from the Continent (wine, cheese, baguettes, mushrooms, etc.); it became a quite common for these to be stuffed into the nose of the aircraft and for the bread to still be hot when it reached bakery shelves in the Islands after the flight from France. By 1979, Aurigny had carried its 2,000,000th passenger, a Mrs Eileen Hodson.

However, competition was never far off. From 1975 to 1980, a rival company sprang up in Alderney to try to supersede Aurigny. Peter Moss was a New Forest man with wide interests (he was everything from a builder to chairman of the Alderney Week committee), who founded Alderney Air Charter with the intention of running scheduled services. He had come over from England having run a failed building business, which he transferred to Alderney. As well as this, he had run a paint shop and to import the paint, a Cessna 336 had been acquired.

However, he found that this was more difficult than he had previously thought and, as a result, it soon evolved into less of a threat to Aurigny, that is, an associate company named Mossair. It operated a fleet of a varying number of the Cessna Skymaster series (Cessna 336s and 337s), usually seven or eight. These were known to the public as 'those funny bucket planes', and the airline had a notorious maintenance record with all the aircraft sometimes being out of action. It also had a Cessna 150 for training purposes and an ex-Rolls Royce de Havilland Dove, which spent some time based at Biggin Hill.

On one flight, a Skymaster's propeller blade sheared off, slicing neatly through one of its tail booms. It limped back to Alderney with the tail hanging off on one side but landed safely, only to have the tail section swapped with that of another un-airworthy aircraft. Because the section was registered to the other aircraft, only half of the Skymaster was airworthy.

The airline made most of its earnings from a valuable contract flying lorry drivers from Cherbourg to Bournemouth. In those days, lorry-carrying ships could only carry twelve people aboard so while the lorry crossed the channel to the UK, those drivers who needed to catch up and re-join their lorry at the end of its voyage would be ferried over by Alderney Air Charter, who would typically fly from Alderney to Cherbourg to pick up the drivers, then fly to Bournemouth (Hurn) to drop them off, and then fly back to Alderney.

Where Moss shot himself in the foot was when he had aircraft out of action. This in itself did not help the company's image, but it was what he did in response that

Some of Alderney Air Charter's Cessna Skymasters parked up. Note Peter Moss' initials on the tail plane of the nearest aircraft. (*Alderney Museum*)

A Cessna 337 Skymaster of Alderney Air Charter flying over the sea, as seen from a boat off the Quesnard area of the island. (*Alderney Museum*)

generated the real problem. According to a well known Alderney pilot, Moss would hire an expensive, gleaming aircraft from a Jersey charter company, and even those without any knowledge whatsoever of aviation could tell the difference between a battered old Skymaster and a gleaming new executive prop. The reason this was an ill-advised decision was that drivers then went straight to the larger charter companies to get nicer aircraft for approximately the same price, severely narrowing Moss' market. The airline went under around 1980.

Meanwhile, Aurigny had had its first incident, which occurred in the mid-1970s: an engine fire in one of the Trislanders on the ground at Guernsey with no one in it. The company have been highly skilled (and lucky) over the years, resulting in very few accidents, due to good maintenance and good care and attention towards their aircraft and pilots.

But back in Alderney, competition was stirring again, posing yet another threat to Aurigny.

Chapter 5
1981-2000

During the next two decades, Alderney aviation changed little, although Aurigny were threatened by a competitor that attempted to take the airline head on; and yet they continued to go from strength to strength.

In 1980, an Aurigny pilot, Captain Martyn Steward, went to the Falkland Islands to train pilots and staff to fly and maintain the Islander aircraft as they were starting a new inter-island government-funded aircraft service, which is, at time of writing, still operating albeit in a slightly different form.

The year 1980 also saw Guernsey with its VOR navigational aid installed and the airway (flight path) rerouted over it, mainly for the benefit of aircraft going to and coming from Heathrow. This resulted in the Alderney equipment no longer being of any further use. Rather than have two expensive-to-run navigation aids of the same type in the bailiwick, the Alderney VOR was decommissioned and is now stored at the Science Museum facility at Wroughton, Wiltshire.

In April 1981, Aurigny published their first edition of *En Voyage*, the in-flight magazine, which was sixteen pages long, and the author and illustrator Peter Seabourne published the first book about Joey ('Joey' being the Channel Islanders' affectionate nickname for the Trislanders). It sold hundreds of copies in the following year and it and other books in the series continue to be sold to this day, except No. 3, which is a collector's item.

The result of this series of books was a fully fledged 'Joey Club', now boasting 2,000 members all under the age of twelve. (At time of writing, there is still a page for the Joey Club in each edition of *En Voyage*.) Over the years, a variety of merchandise has been sold by the Club at Alderney Airport, including t-shirts, sweatshirts and baseball caps.

However, it is not just smiley faces which have featured on Aurigny's aircraft. G-JOEY has worn a giant Santa hat at Christmas and another Trislander – registered G-RBSI – once sported a Loch Ness monster on its nose in a charity campaign.

Also in 1981, battery runway lights were supplied to replace the goose neck flares, both types of which had given firemen the much hated winter task of laying out the lights manually. The mains lighting was only installed as late as 1989. It was renewed in 2006.

Aurigny's first issue of *En Voyage* magazine was published in 1981 with just sixteen pages – a far cry from the rich and glossy periodical that we see today. (*Peter Roberts*)

Alderney Air Ferries advertised day trips to the island from Bournemouth with the incentive of cheap whisky and no VAT. (*Peter Roberts*)

Back in 1979, competition arose again in the shape of Alderney Air Ferries (AAF), which used Britten-Norman Islanders. One of these ran out of fuel and landed two miles short of Bournemouth Airport when returning from Alderney in 1980 because the pilot had not calculated correctly how much fuel he would need. Ronald Ashley was the original founder of AAF, but in 1980 Robin d'Erlanger, a former airline pilot, became CEO of the airline, leading it into different areas of the industry, including expansion – but also administration.

Alderney Air Ferries ran services from Alderney to Bournemouth six times a week, also running an Alderney to Cherbourg service six times a week using Islanders registered G-BESW and G-BEOC. But AAF went bankrupt after G-BEOC's crash-landing at Bournemouth.

Alderney being an island not always keen to conform to what would be considered normal elsewhere in the world, AAF was not going to be run and paid for in the same way as a traditional airline. Sure enough, the airline was owned by subscribers with a minimum of 300 one-pound shares.

The company evolved substantially with new management into Metropolitan Airways in 1982. At the same time as still operating the Bournemouth–Alderney and Cherbourg sectors, it also took over the previous Dan Air 'link city' services from Bournemouth to Manchester and Newcastle.

The northern sectors expanded in 1984 to include Leeds and Glasgow but the southern sectors to Alderney and Cherbourg were dropped, partly because it was now operating bigger aircraft, such as the 35-seat Shorts 330 on lease arrangements from larger companies. Aurigny then took over their Bournemouth sector in 1984, and Metropolitan Airways finally collapsed at the end of summer 1985.

In 1982, the Southampton to Alderney service with Aurigny had continued to be popular, transporting 2,000 passengers that year. The following year, the first Chief Pilot of Aurigny, Bert Lane, retired after flying Trislanders and Islanders for the past 14 years.

Aurigny have supported the Alderney community for over forty years in several ways. As well as being an aerial bus service, it has also carried out all of the medical evacuation flights. This is a highly crucial and sophisticated operation; for when a patient develops an ailment too complex for the hospital on the island, they are flown to Guernsey for treatment there. If this aerial link did not exist, patients would be unable to get quickly from one island to the other at short notice; the airline therefore saves lives.

When one of these flights has to take place at night (there are usually 30-50 medical evacuations a year), certain procedures must be undertaken. The hospital firstly contacts the Aurigny operations officer, who is on constant standby for such eventualities. Contact is then made with Guernsey authorities, who then start a series of 'wake-up' calls. The air traffic controllers and fire officers in both Alderney and Guernsey are given calls to alert them and get the airfields ready for operation. Guernsey negotiate directly with the control centre at Brest in France to open up airspace, and the operations officer in Alderney contacts the ground staff and the pilot to wake them up; they have to prepare the aircraft for the flight, removing seats to change the interior of the aircraft to medical stretcher configuration. There are many people to be woken up, all of whom are part of a slick operation that over the years has saved many lives and has resulted in the safe delivery of many babies. Alderney airport usually remains open until the aircraft returns, as of course it may be needed again that night.

A Britten-Norman Islander parked at Alderney Airport at the launch of Alderney Air Ferries in the late 1970s. (*Alderney Museum*)

During the mid-1980s, Aurigny also took on two de Havilland Twin Otters as a trial scheme, G-BFGP and G-BIMW. The former came from Brymon Airways, an airline from the southwest of England that was phasing them out in favour of the larger and more comfortable de Havilland Dash 7s and Dash 8s. This particular Twin Otter had been operated to the Scilly Isles (St Mary's) from various south-western destinations and Aurigny actually operated the aircraft on the same routes for a short period afterwards – these routes were usually operated by the Islanders, however. G-BIMW came directly from the de Havilland production line in Canada.

The Twin Otters were ultimately unsuccessful as the number of engine start cycles was very high because of the short flight times associated with inter-island sectors. Because this effectively reduced the life of the engines, it resulted in much higher maintenance costs. They flew from Alderney to Shoreham (supplementing Trislanders on this route) and Guernsey, and between there and the mainland.

In 1984, Aurigny took on a new Managing Director, Craig Alexander, who guided it through the competitive times to come, for in 1986, two completely different airlines arrived from south-western England.

Tony Tucker was a Somerset businessman and mayor of Wincanton with a furniture shop and travel agency in the High Street there, as well as having interests in Aviation West. He subsequently started Air Camelot in Alderney. He was a real entrepreneur at heart, later buying Brutonian Buses at the time of bus deregulation in 1986. Nobody could ever say he kept all his eggs in one basket.

Air Camelot was associated with Aviation West in Bristol, and both Air Camelot and Aviation West were owned by Avon Aviation Services who were in liquidation by 1990. It owned a single Trislander and operated basic pattern of rotations of Bristol–Bournemouth–Alderney and then either Alderney–Exeter, or Alderney–Cherbourg. Air Camelot ceased operations after the summer season of 1986, never to be seen again, much to Aurigny's relief.

Regency Airways took over the Air Camelot business and were due to fly Bournemouth–Alderney or Cherbourg from March 1987. But it never flew, failing before it even took off. The airline had even purchased an aircraft, a Trislander registered G-OREG, but this was acquired by Willow Air after their demise. Unfortunately, timetables had been printed, reservations made, and money had changed hands, so it came as quite a shock to those who had been involved when the airline, so close to operating the service, was shut down.

But back in 1985, it was a year of celebrations. Both Alderney Week and the 50th anniversary of the airport brought special visitors: the Red Devils parachute squad performed at Alderney Week while a de Havilland Rapide that flew from the island when the airport was first opened was also present at the celebrations. Wilma Bragg (*née* Wilma Le Cocq, the former airfield controller) also attended. Furthermore, Elizabeth Beresford, Alderney resident and creator of *The Wombles*, wrote an amusing play named *Airport '35*, which told a fictitious story of how the airport came about.

A set of commemorative stamps was also produced, depicting several scenes at the airport including a Trislander, a de Havilland Heron, a Westland Whirlwind helicopter and a de Havilland Rapide. The stamps were not a one-off, as in 1995 another set of aviation-related stamps was released and 2003 saw more stamps (though not as Alderney-specific) produced with the theme of a history of aviation. The year 2008 saw the production of a set relating to Aurigny's 40th anniversary and another set was released in 2009 which commemorated naval aviation, depicting aircraft used by the Royal Navy with Alderney in the background. In 2010, to mark the 70th anniversary of the Battle of Britain, a set of stamps was released that showed a Spitfire soaring above the white cliffs of Dover.

Returning to 1985, it was also the year that an Exeter-based airline was due to make an appearance. The newly formed Jersey European Airlines (now Flybe) had come about from the merger of Air Intra, a Jersey-based airline, and Spacegrand Airlines of Blackpool, organised by Jack Walker, an entrepreneur who owned a raw materials company, Walkersteel Group. JEA had planned to use a de Havilland Twin Otter to fly from Alderney to Shoreham. However, from what can be ascertained from former employees and residents of the island, the route never came about and even though the airline got as far as even putting out a press release about the route, it was never flown.

A couple of years later, in 1987, there was another aviation innovation – Aurigny was the first airline to corporately register their aircraft with the appropriate registrations (such as G-OTSB, G-FTSE or G-XTOR relating to its parent company at that time, Exxtor Group). Meanwhile, they also bought out Guernsey Airlines in 1988, giving them the airline links to Aberdeen, Edinburgh, Glasgow, Cambridge, Southend, Humberside, Zurich, Newcastle, Gloucester, Gatwick and Manchester. They used Vickers Viscounts and Shorts 330s, 70 and 30-seater turboprop aircraft respectively. Aurigny's ideal in

G-AGSH paid a visit to Alderney in 1985 as part of the airport's fiftieth anniversary celebrations. It had flown to the island with Channel Islands Airways after the Second World War but also with BEA during the 1950s. (*Bill Teasdale*)

The Red Devils at Alderney Week 1985, jumping out of their Britten-Norman Islander. (*Alderney Museum*)

the 1980s was that small was good – the airline was still little more than an aerial bus service – so it soon reduced Guernsey Airlines' size, selling the remnants to Air Europe, and ploughing the company's profits back into the airline.

But it was not just Channel Islands airlines that faced ruthless competition. In 1988, another flying club had been formed on Alderney – an alternative to the now firmly established Alderney Flying Club. Ron Wakefield, owner of the Devereux Country House Hotel in Val Fontaine had set up Stratair and parallel company Stratair Engineering (Alderney) Ltd., as a flight training club with the advantage that pilots could secure cheap accommodation. Stratair Flying School started with a Cherokee 140, Cherokee Six and a twin-engined Aztec, all built by Piper in the USA, before expanding in 1990 by adding five twin-seater Tomahawk aircraft to the fleet.

According to one visitor who stayed there, 'It was great fun sharing a hotel with loads of other pilots. The gesticulations of planes doing this or that after dinner or in the bar were hilarious.' He did some training at the flying school and also remembered 'seeing a Stratair instructor running down the road in the headlights of the mini-bus trying to catch a rabbit with the mini-bus full of flying students looking askance at the thought they would be flying with this nutter!' But the fun didn't last and the flying school had shut by the mid-1990s.

March 1988 saw a new flying training school set up on Alderney alongside Stratair and the Alderney Flying Club. Sally Williamson, a qualified nurse, set up Alderney Flying Training with one Cessna 152. It was soon a regular feature for the *Alderney Journal* to show who had recently acquired their Private Pilot's Licence. However, Alderney Flying Training had been discontinued by September 1990 as Williamson, having gained enough hours, decided to pursue her career as a First Officer with Aurigny on its new Shorts 360 aircraft.

Turning its Trislanders into flying billboards with advertisements for local companies was another source of profit for Aurigny, much needed when running any regional airline due to them being indisputably the most unprofitable type of carrier. Meanwhile, it celebrated its 20th anniversary in 1988 by painting a red nose on G-JOEY to coincide with BBC's first ever Comic Relief. Two years later, expansion was continuing at the airline, which introduced the Shorts 360 (otherwise known, affectionately, as 'The Shed' due to its boxy shape), a 36-seat aircraft that flew the Guernsey–London and Manchester sectors. It was adopted from their newly acquired and amalgamated competitor Guernsey Airlines, who had also leased a Vickers Viscount from their parent company, British Air Ferries, to fly on their Guernsey–Gatwick flights.

There were still unforeseen dangers to Alderney tourism, even by February 1986. For the first time in twenty-five years, the runway was shut due to waterlogging, which led to the final stage of widening of the tarmac centre section in 1989.

That same year, another competitor arrived in the shape of Air Sarnia. The airline, a Guernsey-based operator, used two Trislanders registered G-SARN and G-BEFP. It also had an Islander registered quite appropriately G-UERN, and operated in various Alderney sectors, including to Southampton.

It had eventually gained permission to run its routes after a huge row in which Aurigny had objected to the CAA. Air Sarnia, in response, had advertised in both Guernsey and Alderney newspapers that everybody was welcome at the hearing: it wanted as many members of the public as possible to pressurise its competitor.

The runway before (above) and after (below) the widening of the central tarmac strip in 1989. (*Geoff Jones and Ian Haskell respectively*)

Before 1990, when Air Sarnia did get permission to operate scheduled services, it had run as a charter company, with the intention of flying from Alderney to Guernsey and Bembridge (Isle of Wight), and also from Bembridge to Southampton, as well as Southampton to Alderney and Birmingham as scheduled services. The company was granted permission for some of these routes, but never ran the Alderney–Bembridge service.

There were some legal absurdities: the Guernsey authorities, having some problems enforcing their airport charges on Air Sarnia, enlisted Guernsey Police to take whatever action they believed was would force the airline to pay up. Somebody, somewhere in the force, had a bright idea and a civil servant came up with a plan that nobody was expecting. So, on 11 May 1990, Guernsey Police arrested Air Sarnia Trislander G-SARN. They chose to arrest – not impound – the aircraft rather than its pilot, occupants or anyone associated with the airline, claiming that landing and parking fees at Guernsey and Alderney had not been paid, amounting to an £8,800 debt. The Jersey authorities were having similar problems but decided to be slightly more sensible about the matter.

Air Sarnia went bankrupt in late 1990 due to operational costs, and it basically could not keep up with Aurigny's popularity and reputation. Had the airline arrived a decade later, maybe it would have found a foothold.

One of Air Sarnia's Trislanders, G-SARN. The company also had an Islander registered G-UERN. (*Richard Hunt*)

Aurigny were not immune to difficulties either: in 1989 they had a bad financial year due to the strong competition they faced from Air Sarnia. Although it may seem that Aurigny's flights were of a routine and mundane nature, there were some interesting ones, including an in-flight wedding on a chartered Trislander. This took place in 1990 between Wes Donaldson and the Baroness Marlene Schubert who were married by Alderney's Clerk of the States, David Jenkins, at 2,000 feet above the sea near Sark.

In 1991, Aurigny stood in and ran the Guernsey to Gatwick route for a few weeks when Air Europe, the airline who had purchased Guernsey Airlines from Aurigny four years previously, went into administration. It also started to use Trislanders to operate the Guernsey–Dinard route vacated by the now defunct Air Sarnia.

It was clear that Aurigny was set to expand, and this was proved when it landed a profitable contract with Guernsey Post in 1992 to carry all the mail from the UK. Aurigny still carries the mail over to Alderney by Trislander, taking the seats out and putting them back in again like a modified hatchback with wings.

Aurigny celebrated its 25th anniversary in 1993 with a re-enactment of the first Alderney to Guernsey flight on 1 March and, in 1994, the 2,500,000th passenger passed through Alderney Airport since records began in 1949. He was presented with a bottle of champagne and, rather surprisingly, a cardigan.

In 1995, Alderney Airport obtained its own refueller and refuelling tanks, administered by Cyma Petroleum, for supplying 100LL (low lead) Avgas. However, the arrangement fell apart in 2005 when the storage facilities were deemed unsafe during a States health and safety inspection. This deterred private pilots from coming to the island and caused problems for both Aurigny and Le Cocq's Airlink – both airlines would have to refuel in Guernsey. This lack of fuel was, for the greater part, also responsible for the demise of the Alderney Fly-In after a twenty-year run of success. The fuel facilities were later restored to their present condition, administered instead by Alderney Electricity.

There is a distinct advantage to buying fuel on the island: it is duty-free. At time of writing, it is still economical for some pilots based in the south and southwest of England with a large fuel tank capacity to fly to Alderney to fill their tanks, saving larger sums of money on the duty-free fuel than they spend flying over.

The year 1995 also saw the former Hawker employee Alec Clark and the joint founder of Britten-Norman, Desmond Norman, announce that a Trislander derivative was to be built in Belgium, named the Clark-Norman Triloader. The aircraft would be entirely for freight transport and would have STOL capability, with hopes that it could be in production by late 1998. However, there was insufficient funding for the project as Clark-Norman failed to find the backing of a larger company.

Aurigny unveiled new markings in 1996 on the side of all of its aircraft although five Trislanders later swapped their Aurigny colours for those of corporate sponsors turning them into flying billboards. The last of Aurigny's corporate colour schemes was phased out in April 2009. G-RLON had worn the colours of Royal London Asset Management for more than half a decade (quite a long time for an advertisement) and the time for it to have Aurigny's normal colours applied was when the door on its nose fell off on an inter-island flight in 2009. Fortunately, it returned to Jersey unscathed. Subsequent investigation revealed that a fatigued latching mechanism had caused the problem.

Back in Alderney, in 1997, the Alderney Air Races took place for the first time following many months of negotiations with both the States of Alderney and the States of Guernsey. Taking place annually in late September, the Races were at first grouped as counting for the first points of the next season. This has since changed and they are now the key races in determining the Royal Aero Club British Air Racing Champion, the European Air Race Champion as well as many other air racing trophies. The event attracts somewhere in the region of thirty aircraft each year.

Aurigny further expanded their fleet in 1999, using Saab 340 aircraft to fly from Guernsey to London Stansted. This was the start of the evolution from a basic aerial bus service to the fully-fledged regional airline that Aurigny is today. It also began a relatively short-lived Guernsey–Amsterdam service. The year 1999 also saw Alderney Flying Training replace its Cessna 152s (sold to, and subsequently flown as training aircraft by, Guernsey Aero Club) with a Piper PA-28-181 Archer II aircraft, which was transferred from the Dutch register and re-registered in the UK as G-BXRG. Alderney Flying Training, along with its affiliate association Alderney Flying Club, had been running for about fifteen years beforehand, with the former providing pilot training to anyone who needed it, and the latter being a club with a solely social purpose, as well as letting members rent G-BXRG for flights of their own.

The briefing before Alderney Air Races, inside the airport hangar. (*Geoff Jones*)

The Piper Archer II of Alderney Flying Club, registered G-BXRG, on finals to the westerly runway. The club acquired the aircraft from the Netherlands in 1999. (*Author's own collection*)

Chapter 6
2001-Present

In 1999, Le Cocq's Stores, the local supermarket, had begun flying fresh produce into Alderney from the UK. The aircraft used for the Alderney–Bournemouth and Alderney–Shoreham operation was noticed by local residents who were not happy with Aurigny's rising prices. Some believed that Aurigny were taking advantage of having the monopoly on the entirety of island air links and consequently keeping prices as high as they dared. Residents would have little option but to use the airline if they wished to get off the island due to a lack of scheduled ferry links. They therefore asked Noel Hayes, owner of Le Cocq's and the aircraft, if he could carry passengers on the aircraft he was using to fly in produce, to go to the mainland the other islands.

After a good deal of preparation, AirX Ltd. (trading as Le Cocq's Airlink) was born. It operated one Britten-Norman Islander, appropriately registered G-XAXA, and later another, G-BIIP which for part of 2000 and 2001 was brightly coloured (blue, purple, orange and white-striped) as it had recently been received from Air Express in Jamaica. Later painted in Le Cocq's colours, the aircraft flew daily to Guernsey, Jersey, Bournemouth and later Shoreham, which became a popular service.

In 2001, Le Cocq's Airlink was renamed and rebranded Rockhopper, and in the same year another Britten-Norman Trislander, registered G-LCOC, was acquired. This aircraft was the subject of quite an interesting incident in September 1986 under the ownership of Kondair, a cargo and freight airline with three Trislanders, G-LCOC (then registered G-BCCU) being one of them.

The pilot was flying from Amsterdam Schiphol to London Stansted at 1,000 feet. He nodded off halfway through his journey and woke up ten minutes later. He fell asleep again soon after, but this time the consequences of his lack of attention were somewhat worse. He was leaning forward on the control column so the aircraft had started to descend. He only woke up when the wheels were brushing the surface of the North Sea and so he took evasive action (albeit probably quite dozily) and climbed back to 1,000 feet. When he looked out of the window to check for external damage, he noticed that the right wheels were missing but managed to land safely at London Stansted, his lesson learnt.

Twenty years later, the same aircraft was operating for Rockhopper on daily services from Alderney to Guernsey, Jersey, Bournemouth and Shoreham (Brighton City) – this

Le Cocq's Airlink acquired a Trislander in direct competition with Aurigny's longstanding aerial bus service. The airline was an immediate success as some islanders felt that new blood was needed to drive prices down. (*Geoff Jones*)

was proving to be a profitable operation and one which favoured expansion. It was the first real threat to Aurigny since Air Sarnia had burst in, shattering their monopoly.

In 2000, Alderney entered the virtual flying world – Microsoft had started producing flight simulator computer programmes that included the island. It was featured in their Flight Simulator series in 2000, 2002, 2004 and X, their tenth flight simulator. It has become more realistic throughout each edition. In Flight Simulator 2000, a river ran under the airport, while in Flight Simulator 2002 the sea was shown climbing up the cliffs to the south; but the latest edition depicts the island more or less correctly.

Earth Simulations has made some highly acclaimed scenery of Alderney as an upgrade for Flight Simulator X, the present edition of the program, and it has been nominated as some of the most convincing Flight Simulator scenery of all time. The Trislander (long nose variant), meanwhile, has been available as a downloadable add-on for Microsoft Flight Simulator since their 1997 edition (Flight Simulator 98), and a short nose version is available for a competitor flight simulator, XPlane.

Back in reality, in late 2001, security checks were introduced after the September 11th attacks in New York, and the security facilities are checked by the CAA and DfT. It is interesting to note that these security measures are imposed by the Guernsey Airport administration, as it is not a requirement to have such a security facility at an airport where operating aircraft do not exceed ten metric tonnes in weight and have a seating capacity of less than nineteen seats (as is also the case in the Scilly Isles).

Blue Islands' Trislander, G-LCOC, about to take off from Alderney's Runway 26. The same aircraft had a close shave with the North Sea in 1986. (*Author's own collection*)

Aurigny acquired one ATR 72–200 in 2003, a 60-seater aircraft, registered G-BXTN (formerly owned by British Airways, who in turn had acquired it from CityFlyer when BA bought out the airline). This aircraft inaugurated operations one day after British Airways dropped the Guernsey–Gatwick route, continuing Guernsey's lifeline London link.

The airline also leased a BAe 146 from Titan Airways for various summer weekends from 2000 to 2005, as well as a Boeing 737-300 from the same operator to fill in for the ATR–72 when it was unserviceable. Aurigny's charter capacity was growing with summer flights to Cambridge (Teversham), Gloucestershire (Staverton), Southend (Rochford) and Manston (Kent International) in addition to various other destinations depending on demand from travel companies.

Having seen Air UK drop the lifeline Guernsey–Heathrow route in 1998 after its acquisition by KLM, the States of Guernsey were well aware how vulnerable the islands' air links were. When British Airways announced the closure of the Guernsey–Gatwick route, the States started to get agitated as airlines could drop their less profitable routes to London airports and get millions of pounds for the slots. (Airlines must buy slot times at busier airports, which at London airports are worth hundreds of thousands of pounds.) So the States did what they thought was logical and bought Aurigny Air Services from Close Brothers Private Equity in a deal worth £5 million. This would then secure Guernsey's air routes in years to come – and it appears to have worked.

The ATR also helped to ease the tight turnarounds imposed on the 3 Saab 340 and Shorts 360 aircraft that the airline was using. Aurigny also used their newly acquired capacity to start routes from Guernsey to Bristol and Jersey to Stansted.

The CAA ran a project in 2003 to consult private aircraft pilots as to what could be done to avoid airspace infringement. The conclusion of this was that it would be rather helpful if Alderney were to install a new generation, low-cost VOR or DME (navigational devices similar to the one decommissioned on the island in 1980) to help when Channel Islands airspace was busy, for example on summer weekends. This was not deemed cost effective, however, so the idea came to nothing.

Rockhopper expanded fast having received huge demand on its routes and soon acquired its second Trislander, registered G-RHOP, and then a third, G-BEDP, received from Lydd Air on the Kent coast. G-RHOP was another of Rockhopper's aircraft that had a somewhat iffy history. It had flown with Kondair (registered as G-BEFP), based at Stansted at the same time as G-LCOC, and its sister ship G-BDTP had crashed while on final approach to Amsterdam (Schiphol) in September 1986, resulting in the tragic death of the pilot as the aircraft turned and side-slipped into the ground. However, before its acquisition by Rockhopper, G-RHOP had been owned by a charter company, and registered as G-WEAC. On 28 January 2000, it was being flown on a late night flight from Edinburgh to Belfast (Aldergrove) by a pilot who was somewhat inexperienced with the Trislander, having only flown thirty-eight hours on this type of aircraft. He carried no passengers and took off late that evening.

After takeoff, the aircraft entered cloud at 2,500 feet, and the pilot selected propeller de-ice and windscreen heat. At 3,500 feet, he noticed large accumulations of ice on the wings and a quarter of an inch of ice on the windscreen. The significance of this is that ice on the wings of an aircraft means a loss of lift, so it can topple out of the sky. All anti-icing systems were switched on but, at 4,300 feet, the rate of climb was zero. The pilot applied full engine power but to no avail, so in accordance with the operating manual he applied ten degrees of flap (flaps are hinged surfaces on the back of the wing that increase the lift of the aircraft but also decrease the speed). For a while this helped, but the aircraft soon started to descend once again. Ice was not being dislodged and the aircraft was starting to lose altitude at a higher rate. At 2,000 feet, the pilot requested an emergency diversion to Prestwick. Mountainous areas and thick cloud meant that the conditions could not be withstood for long. Scottish Air Traffic Control Centre, who had guided him through the more hilly areas at his inherently unsafe altitude, handed over control to Prestwick Air Traffic Control when he was 4.6 miles from the airport at a height of 900 feet. He miraculously managed to maintain altitude for the remaining distance and finally landed at 1.22 a.m.

The episode was, according to the AAIB, 'a potentially catastrophic incident that was averted by good fortune and the actions of ATC controllers'. The conclusion of the subsequent investigation was that the aircraft's anti-icing systems had partially failed, resulting in the reduced performance because of ice build-up on the wings and body of the aircraft. The pilot's inexperience was not deemed to be a contributing factor in the accident.

After Rockhopper acquired this plucky little Trislander, it leased a further two Islanders from Hebridean Air Services over the next few years as well as purchasing another. It opened new routes from Guernsey to St Brieuc and from Alderney to Cherbourg (reportedly only ever flown on one scheduled air service after the 9/11 atrocities).

In February 2006, Rockhopper was rebranded. As Blue Islands was the airline's call sign, it seemed the obvious new name. This was quite fortunate given that a Rockhopper is a type of penguin which, of course, cannot fly. The rebranding exercise coincided with the acquisition of three British Aerospace (BAe) Jetstreams, and the 100 per cent share being bought by Healthspan, a Guernsey company that manufactures health products as well as owning hotels throughout the Channel Islands.

At around this time, a new airline on the Isle of Wight, named rather imaginatively Wight Airlines, had started flying from Sandown to London City using a Piper Navajo in 8-seat configuration. If it had not gone bankrupt within the first month of operation, it would have also started a Guernsey–Alderney–London City route, with a whistle-stop in Sandown. The licence was approved in August 2006; however, the Channel Islands services came to nothing as the airline could not make a profit, never maintaining any kind of feasibility, and going bankrupt shortly afterwards.

Also in 2006, the runway lights at Alderney were replaced with new high-intensity lighting. Ian Tugby dug the trenches at the sides of the runway for the lights.

Soon, Blue Islands had opened new routes from Jersey to the Isle of Man and from Guernsey to Cardiff. However, the Cardiff route was soon dropped due to lack of demand, a reason so often cited by the airline. The St Brieuc route was retained but now utilised the new BAe Jetstreams.

The year 2007 saw further expansion at Blue Islands with the opening of a new air route from Jersey to Paris operated by the Jetstreams. The following year, the airline cut the Alderney–Shoreham route, leaving passengers either stranded or put on flights to Bournemouth. This served as a blow to islanders and visitors alike. Although the airline was lessening its focus on Alderney and moving further towards regional airline operations from Jersey and Guernsey, this was not the sole reason for the end of the Shoreham link. The route had started off as a daily service, then moved to a less regular schedule of three or four times a week. It was then downgraded further to only two flights a week. However, schedules were increased to four flights per week shortly before the route's closure, probably in an attempt to inspire demand.

At first, load factors had not been bad but as the novelty of the route wore off, passenger numbers took a dive until during its last winter of operation; the route was sometimes only carrying one person per flight – blatantly an unprofitable operation. Lack of interest has long been a problem blighting new air links to the island, and the Shoreham service did not buck the trend for long.

Thus, Alderney had its southeast England connection cut, something that did not go unnoticed. Travellers would now have to go to either Southampton or Bournemouth, and then catch a train to central London. By 2008, Blue Islands had returned two of its four Islanders to Hebridean Air Services, who were leasing them to the airline. Blue Islands also sold G-BIIP, retaining their first aircraft, Islander G-XAXA which, at time of writing, remains with the airline and is used for training, charters and scheduled flights. The airline then brought in an Alderney–Jersey direct service over that summer, probably to make amends with islanders, but they had dropped the route by late autumn.

Aurigny had ceased operation on the route when Blue Islands started competing as they considered that it would be unprofitable with two competing operators. Unfortunately, this left the island without its link to Jersey, a service which, at time of writing, has not been replaced. It also leased a Dornier 328 from ScotAirways and initiated services from Jersey to Geneva and Zurich.

Meanwhile, Aurigny's main competition in Guernsey, Flybe, launched an online campaign against them in March 2008 in which it compared its 'professional 78-seater' aircraft with Aurigny's 'small aircraft called Joey'. It also attacked their competitor on the grounds that it had not added any new routes since 2005, and that its aircraft were both more environmentally unfriendly and older than those operated by Flybe.

However, all this was changed in 2009 when Aurigny added two new routes and took delivery of some new aircraft in the form of two ATR 72-500s. These are more environmentally friendly and newer than Flybe's Dash 8s. Aurigny's commercial director, Malcolm Coupar, put a remarkable spin on Flybe's accusation, saying: 'As for Joey, thousands of children have grown up with him and he's a character that many islanders hold close to their hearts. Only a bully would pick on him.' This was rather more than Flybe had bargained for. Coupar also said that: 'The Britten-Norman Trislander has an excellent and proven track record and we are proud that they remain in our fleet.' He then put Aurigny's competitor firmly in its place by pointing out that 'Flybe, by its own claim, is Europe's largest low-cost regional airline. It carried more than seven million passengers in 2007 and collected more than £500 million in revenues. This makes it around twenty times the size of Aurigny ... it seems strange that Flybe would spend so much of its time on criticising a smaller airline.'

Back in Alderney the following year, another Blue Islands route was cut, which meant that routes became yet more limited from the island, leading customers to speculate as to whether Blue Islands would pull out of Alderney completely. In February 2009, it dropped both the Alderney–Bournemouth and Guernsey–Bournemouth routes, citing low demand and leaving Alderney with just one route to the UK mainland and Aurigny with the monopoly, which was the exact reason that Blue Islands was started in the first place. The cut disappointed some Alderney residents as well as made accessibility to the island a good deal more complex for holidaymakers who had previously travelled with the airline.

Due to tourism being Alderney's main source of income, the lack of air links have worried States members and there were suggestions in March 2010 that Aurigny could run new routes from the island to the mainland, subsidised by the States of Guernsey. But, at time of writing, no further progress has been made.

However, Blue Islands then implemented a Southampton to Alderney flight connection via Guernsey, which at least leaves the passenger the choice of whether to fly direct on Aurigny or have a longer journey time and stopover with Blue Islands.

Later that year, Blue Islands expanded into Europe: in July 2009, it leased one 46-seat ATR 42-320 to fly its Switzerland routes as a trial to see if larger capacity was wanted. The trial was popular so G-DRFC, the oldest aircraft of its type still flying, was employed in permanent use on the routes. The company stated that this was the beginning of a large fleet refurbishment with new routes to be added subsequently – a large expansion. Due to difficult economic conditions, no new routes were launched for a considerable amount of time after this.

Routes operated by Jersey Airlines

Welcome Aboard !

.   .   .   on any section of the Jersey Airlines network

Next time **YOU** travel on any of these routes, make a point of flying by Jersey Airlines.

The vigorous expansion of this great airline is the result of its policy of treating the individual passenger's safety and comfort as its first and fundamental concern

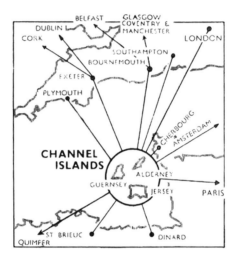

Services between CHANNEL ISLANDS and:-

London	Cork
Bournemouth	Dublin
Southampton	Dinard
Exeter	Cherbourg
Plymouth	Paris
Coventry	St. Brieuc
Manchester	Quimper
Glasgow	Amsterdam

Connections can also be made between any of these places via the Channel Islands

Some other direct Jersey Airlines Services:-

Manchester – Bournemouth	Exeter – Dublin
Belfast – Bournemouth	Exeter – Cork
Exeter – Paris	

Above: Jersey Airlines' 1962 timetable shows the many routes they operated at the time, including from Alderney to Guernsey, Jersey, Gatwick and Bournemouth. (*Peter Roberts*)

Previous page: The Handley Page Herald that visited Alderney on 16 October 1956 is still the largest aircraft to have landed on the island. (*Ralph Burridge*)

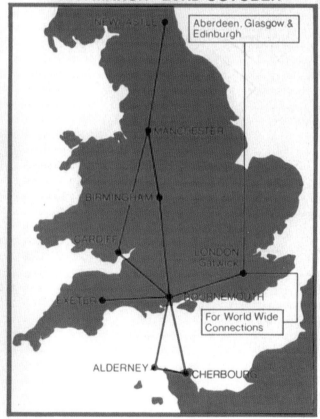

Metropolitan Airways

IN SUCCESSION TO

Alderney Air Ferries

SCHEDULED SERVICES

SUMMER TIMETABLE 1982
29TH MARCH - 23RD OCTOBER

Aberdeen, Glasgow & Edinburgh

For World Wide Connections

OPERATORS OF THE
DAN-AIR LINK-CITY SERVICES

Metropolitan Airways operated in succession to Alderney Air Ferries, in addition to flying many of Dan-Air's inter-UK link-city services. (*Peter Roberts*)

AVIATION WEST

AIR CAMELOT

Scheduled Service

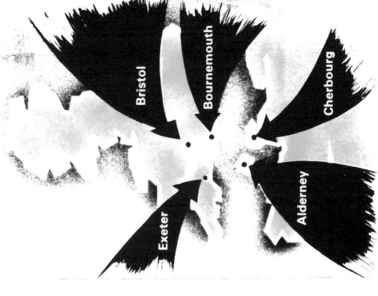

Bristol
Bournemouth
Cherbourg
Exeter
Alderney

TIMETABLE Summer 1986

'Reliable, efficient & FAST'

Aviation West offer a complete air charter service using a fleet of aircraft tailored to meet varying requirements. Chartering an aircraft provides the opportunity for businessmen and organised groups to travel at short notice, in comfort and style.

More often than not, by using smaller airports we can take you closer to your eventual destination than a scheduled flight would, saving you precious time and money.

Return schedules are equally reliable, with the aircraft and pilot at your disposal. Should your plans alter in any way, Aviation West can adjust the flight times to suit.

Flexibility & Choice

Fixed wing or helicopters

Aviation West operates a flexible fleet of aircraft, providing from 4, right up to 17-seat capacity. Through our associate company Aviation West Helicopters, we can offer 4 and 5-seat helicopters for those special charters and filming tasks.

FOR INFORMATION AND QUOTATIONS
Contact: Aviation West Bristol Airport, LULSGATE
Avon BS19 3DY Telex: 444988

GENERAL INFORMATION

FARES on international routes, children under 2 years are carried at 10% of the adult fare, children between 2 years and 12 years inclusive are carried at half the adult fare

UNACCOMPANIED CHILDREN By prior arrangement children between 8 years and 12 years.

INVALIDS Every effort will be made to accommodate disabled, sick or infirm passengers Please consult Air Camelot well in advance as special approval and assistance may be required.

BAGGAGE ALLOWANCE There is no free allowance for infants travelling. For all other passengers the allowance is 15Kgs (33 lbs).

Excess baggage is carried, subject to load and space availability, at the published rate

Each passenger may carry on board a small cabin bag, the weight of which must not exceed 3Kgs

RESTRICTED ARTICLES Government regulations prohibit the carriage of certain articles, such as explosives, compressed gases, radioactive or magnetic materials etc, instruments or articles containing mercury must be so placed as to avoid spillage

FREIGHT We offer a small freight service on all our routes, please contact Air Camelot for further details

ANIMALS Seeing eye dogs, pet cats and dogs may be carried under certain conditions. Please contact Air Camelot for further details.

AIRCRAFT TYPE The carrier reserves the right to alter the aircraft type without prior notification.

CANCELLATION AND NO-SHOW CHARGES A passenger failing either to cancel his/her reservation, or to check-in in time to join the flight on which he/she is booked, may incur a forfeiture of 100%

WEATHER Please note that Air Camelot cannot be held responsible for any delays due to weather conditions

PUNCTUALITY Every effort is made to ensure punctuality and regularity of our services. Air Camelot cannot accept responsibility for any consequence arising, as a result of delay to, or a cancellation of, any services due to circumstances beyond our control and cannot guarantee to make connections with the services of other air and surface carriers

Aurigny's de Havilland DHC-6 Twin Otter, seen on the apron at Alderney in May 1980, mostly in the colour scheme of its former operator, Brymon Airways, but with a basic Aurigny title. (*Richard Vandervord*)

Above: One of Alderney Air Ferries' Islanders in May 1980. Note the enthusiastic passenger in the second row. (*Richard Vandervord*)

Opposite: Air Camelot/Aviation West were unperturbed by previous failures to supersede Aurigny; they operated between Alderney and Cherbourg, Bournemouth and Exeter with an indirect service to Bristol. (*Peter Roberts*)

Aurigny's second-last remaining Islander (along with G-AXWP), the others having all been retired, pictured on the tarmac at Alderney in May 1980. (*Richard Vandervord*)

An Aurigny Trislander, registered G-BNCO, taxiing under a cloudless sky in 1980. Aurigny's outlook has not always been as clear, yet the carrier has managed to weather storms that defeated other carriers. (*Richard Vandervord*)

Aurigny's 1990s colour scheme, seen here on G-XTOR. The aircraft also bears the title 'Destination Dinard' to correspond with the airline's routes there. (*Ian Haskell*)

Today, Aurigny is owned by the States of Guernsey, giving it much-needed financial backing in a tough time for airlines, helping it to continue to provide the lifeline links that the Channel Islands depend on. (*Author's own collection*)

Le Cocq's Airlink acquired a Trislander in 2001 in direct competition to Aurigny's long-standing aerial bus service. The airline was an immediate success as some islanders felt that new blood was needed to drive prices down. (*Geoff Jones*)

Le Cocq's Airlink soon evolved into Rockhopper, and founder Noel Hayes (left) is seen here celebrating the rebranding. (*Geoff Jones*)

A Blue Islands Trislander takes flight at dusk. Rockhopper had become Blue Islands in 2006, while the trusty Trislander has been used by nearly all airlines that have operated to Alderney since the mid-1970s. It continues to be a versatile aircraft suited to tackling the island's short runways and challenging approaches. (*Author's own collection*)

Rockhopper's second Trislander, G-RHOP, seen here at Alderney airport in Blue Islands livery on a wet May afternoon in 2007. The aircraft was later exported to New Zealand to fly with Great Barrier Airlines. (*Geoff Jones*)

Some islanders own their own aircraft, such as Richard Herivel with his kit-built Murphy Rebel, registered G-DIKY. (*Geoff Jones*)

Above: Aurigny's Britten Norman Trislander as seen in May 1980, now registered G-JOEY. It is seen here under the guise of G-BDGG, painted in a basic colour scheme. (*Richard Vandervord*)

Opposite: While airlines come and go, the facilities at Alderney Airport, shown here in the present day, have been mostly unaltered since the late 1960s and will probably remain so in the near future. (*Geoff Jones*)

Aurigny's Trislanders have had some strange colour schemes over the years, from an unpainted Trislander nicknamed Snowy Joey to the Loch Ness Monster. Here G-JOEY has a smiley face painted on the aircraft's nose. (*Geoff Jones*)

The Alderney Air Races attract a wide variety of aircraft and pilots each year, including an air traffic controller from the Balearics as well as airmen and women from all over the United Kingdom. (*Geoff Jones*)

Many interesting aircraft have visited Alderney. Here, a French helicopter charter, inbound from Cherbourg, sits on the tarmac. (*Richard Vandervord*)

The Royal Navy continues to use Alderney for various training exercises, not least Search and Rescue operations. (*Geoff Jones*)

The Channel Islands Air Search aircraft, a Britten-Norman Islander registered G-CIAS and named *Lions Pride* after donations from both Guernsey and Jersey branches of the Lions Club. (*Geoff Jones*)

Above: An EADS Socata TBM 700C1, registered N700GY, after its nose gear failure in March 2008, being inspected by the Airfield Fire and Rescue service. (*James Varley*)

Opposite: A Piper PA-32R-300 Cherokee Lance aircraft, registered G-BTCA, after crashing and catching fire in August 2009. The occupants escaped before the blaze. (*James Varley*)

Alderney Week usually sees a massive increase in private aircraft movements, considerably increasing the workload for the air traffic controllers. (*Author's own collection*)

After forty years of service, Trislanders still suit the needs of Alderney, meaning that 'Joey' should continue to grace the island's skies for some years to come. (*Richard Strickland*)

Noel Hayes, founder of Blue Islands, started a new airline in the Isle of Man called Manx2 after selling Blue Islands to Healthspan in 2006, which at time of writing is the premier Isle of Man based operator serving the island since EuroManx went bankrupt in 2008. It actually competes with Blue Islands on the Isle of Man–Jersey route, with the difference that it connects at Gloucestershire Airport (Staverton) as opposed to using Blue Islands' direct route.

January 2010 saw the most snow the airport had seen for many years. This wreaked havoc, as did the ice that followed it. The runway was shut for five days with only a couple of flights managing to limp out of the island. Three JCBs did, however, do a very good job of clearing the snow.

Another stoppage to flights at the airport took place in April 2010 due to a volcanic eruption at Eyjafjallajökull in Iceland, which spewed ash into the atmosphere and a steady north-westerly wind blew the cloud over European airspace. For six days, flights were prohibited to Southampton due to the airport there being shut, although Aurigny did gain special permission to operate on the seventh day, making them the only airline to operate out of Southampton that day. Ash can cause an engine to fail, but piston engines (such as those used in Trislanders) are not usually affected. Inter-island flights continued on a revised schedule.

When the States of Guernsey accounts were filed in May 2010, it emerged that Alderney Airport had made a trading loss of nearly £735,000, which was a 20 per cent greater than the loss the previous year and over 20 per cent above the States estimate of £600,000. Public Services Department were forced to utilise unused money that had been set aside for road maintenance. However, Minister Bernard Flouquet said that in future PSD may have to ask the States for more money as the airport is a lifeline, meaning that cutting it was not an option. Some argued that the airport should be run as a separate entity like Alderney Water, and that its accounting should be clearly published for all to see.

Chapter 7
Notable Accidents and Incidents

Alderney has been quite lucky, with only a couple of serious accidents on the island. It is aided by a well-equipped fire service that is able to tackle any situation that might arise. The Airport Manager, Keith Webster, has commented that Alderney has definitely had its fair share of undercarriage collapses, which have probably been the most common type of incident over the last decade.

PRE-WAR INCIDENTS

There were few incidents in pre-war Alderney, partly due to the lack of a formal airfield until 1936. The first accident took place on *5 October 1919* when two Avro 504L seaplanes were being flown to Jersey. One reached Jersey, but the other became lost in fog and was forced to ditch in the sea near Alderney. This resulted in its being wrecked on the Breakwater as it tried to enter Braye bay.

On *13 October 1923*, a Supermarine Sea Eagle aircraft, flying in a pair with another of the same type, suffered engine problems. Both were owned by the British Marine Navigation Company (BMNC) and landed in rough seas near the Casquets. The other aircraft then landed in Braye harbour and the pilot (Supermarine's Chief Pilot) Henri Biard alerted islanders, who told him there was no boat strong enough on the island to get to the aircraft. It was very windy, gusting force eight, but nevertheless Biard took off again and his aircraft was flung forty feet in the air by a stray wave, damaging the floats and undersides of the boat, and throwing passengers all over the place – one vomited, another was hurled at the box of grapes he was taking back to his wife. A newspaper correspondent wrote a fantastic account of the flight, although it was later established that he had been unconscious for its entirety. Nevertheless, the aircraft got back to St Peter Port safely, and Biard managed to divert a cargo boat heading for Southampton to give assistance. Luckily, an Alderney-based Trinity House launch, *Lita*, saw the stricken aircraft, and the skipper Nick Allen and pilot Dave Ingrouille capsized their dinghy trying to get a tow rope across to the aircraft. They eventually managed to secure it and towed it back to the shelter of Longis Bay until the tide allowed for it to get around to Braye. On 15 October, the stricken Sea Eagle flew to Guernsey for repairs, only to be sunk in St. Peter Port harbour on 15 December 1926 after being accidentally rammed by another boat.

On *29 June 1936*, a de Havilland DH.84 Dragon – named *Rozel Bay* and registered G-ACNJ – owned by Channel Islands Airways, overran the runway at Alderney. The pilot, a Mr Martin, had to circle the airfield twice due to bad visibility, and when he did approach, the aircraft was a little too fast. Martin landed the aircraft, whereupon the brakes failed, or so he claimed. Faced with hitting an earth bank or a herd of six cows, he chose the bank, destroying the starboard propeller and damaging the undercarriage in the process. Nobody was injured and the aircraft was patched up before flying to Eastleigh a week later for more comprehensive repairs.

On *6 April 1939*, a Handley Page Harrow bomber crash landed on the Grande Blaye, bouncing over a hedge and coming to rest on the airfield. Maurice Rick, later to be airfield controller, came to the island to repair the aircraft in August 1939, and it was able to fly off the island a short time before war was declared.

WARTIME INCIDENTS

While every effort has been made to document all accidents and incidents and to do so correctly, it has been somewhat difficult as not all crashes were recorded during the war – this is especially the case with the Luftwaffe. It is therefore highly likely that there were more crashes than are documented here.

On *20 July 1940*, a Heinkel He59, a type of German biplane, of Seenotflug.Kdo.4, crashed near Alderney. Colonel Otto Dreyer claimed to have been machine-gunned by a British bomber while attempting to rescue a stricken Luftwaffe pilot who had been shot down. Dreyer and his crew landed in a dinghy on Alderney, a day after the incident.

On *31 December 1940*, an Arado Ar.196, a German seaplane used by the Kriegsmarine (German Navy), 5./KuFlGr.196, crashed near Alderney. The aircraft was extremely badly damaged after an emergency landing in bad weather. Whether the crew survived or not is unclear; however, it is reputed that one man died and another suffered severe injury.

On *30 October 1941*, a Supermarine Spitfire Mk Vb, W3849 of 118 Squadron, was hit by flak from ships heading for Cherbourg. Piloted by Sergeant Geoffrey Arthur Painting, the aircraft was east of Alderney at the time and came down into the sea in fog. The pilot died on impact.

On *2 November 1941*, a Supermarine Spitfire Mk V, W3830 with squadron code AZ K, crashed on Alderney, having attacked a wireless station at Audeville with four other aircraft. Although the attack was successful and hits were registered on the building, the aircraft later developed engine trouble and crash landed on Alderney. The pilot, Pilot Officer B. W. Meyer of 234 Squadron, was taken as a prisoner of war. He was injured and spent most of November and December 1941 in hospital on Alderney before then being transferred and subsequently hospitalised again at the Stalag Luft III prison camp (the camp to which most captured airmen were sent).

On *8 November 1941*, a Supermarine Spitfire Mk Vb, AD188 with squadron code SD O, had taken off from the mainland at 13.50 with the rest of 501 Squadron to attack a target in France, after the 'Rhubarb' operation (a low-level strike operation performed in cloudy conditions against enemy targets in Occupied Countries) had earlier been aborted due to extremely bad weather. Pilot Officer W. J. H. Greenway, who was flying the aircraft, was attacked by a German Messerschmitt Bf. 109 fighter aircraft, and was seen at 10,000 feet with white smoke coming from the engine, going through a cloud layer. He later crash landed on Alderney and survived, also being transferred to the notorious Stalag Luft III prison camp. He later reported to his son that while on Alderney the Germans had treated him well, keeping him in their headquarters at the Grand Hotel. They would take him out for exercise twice a day, where he would get a chance to meet the few remaining locals and see new fortifications springing up at a rate of knots.

Pilot Officer
W. J. H. Greenway,
who crash landed on
Alderney on
8 November 1941.
He is shown in a
photograph taken
when he joined the
RAF. (*Tim Osborne*)

Sometime during *1941/1942*, a Messerschmitt Bf. 109 crashed on Alderney in the Bonne Terre area of the island. There are conflicting reports as to what happened. One story says that the 109 was being used to drop the mail onto the island and was being flown by a German doctor. At some stage, it suffered a mechanical failure of some kind, and he bailed out. It then apparently crashed, went through a wall, breaking up and eventually came to rest with the wings broken off from the fuselage and leaking large amounts of aviation fuel. The propeller and boss had broken away from the engine, ending up in scrubland some 100 metres away. When the aircraft was partially dismantled, it is reputed that the engine was rolled into the pond at the bottom of the hill. Remnants of the aircraft still remained when islanders returned at the end of 1945 and a burnt area near La Bonne Terre is clearly visible in a 1942 aerial photograph.

On *5 June 1943*, a Supermarine Spitfire Mk Vc, EN953 of 504 Squadron, piloted by Sergeant Gerald Frank Locke crashed into the sea close to Alderney while flying in foggy conditions. The pilot was killed. Little is known about the circumstances of the accident.

On *4 February 1944*, a Hawker Typhoon Mk lb, JP902 'D' of 193 Squadron crashed into the sea following an attack on Cap de la Hague. The aircraft was piloted by Sergeant John Richard King-Meggot (spelt with an 'o' as opposed to an 'a', contrary to some records), of the Royal Air Force Volunteer Reserve, who tragically died in the incident.

On *5 February 1944*, a Hawker Typhoon Mk lb, JR251 of 263 Squadron and piloted by Flight Officer Norman Peter Blacklock, crashed into the sea near Alderney. The aircraft was on a shipping reconnaissance mission to Alderney and Cap de la Hague. The pilot sadly died in the incident.

Sometime during *1944/1945*, an Avro Lancaster crashed into the sea to the west of Alderney. The crew were taken prisoners of war.

POST-WAR INCIDENTS

Due to the huge increase in popularity of private aviation, incidents on the island have inevitably risen, although only few have been serious. Again, due to a lack of written documentation, there may be incidents which have not been included here; however, the author has attempted to collate as many as possible.

On *26 August 1967*, Piper Tripacer, G-ARXK, crashed near Alderney according to *Flight* magazine from September 1967. It stalled on finals to the airfield and fell into the sea 200 yards from the shore. The pilot, Air Commodore C. E. S. Lockett, and his passengers, Dr W. L. James and Lady Ursula James, were drowned. There was no evidence of mechanical failure, but the Inspector of Air Accidents speculated that the aircraft may have suffered a bird strike. This was later found to be the only possible reason as the aircraft probably hit a seagull, causing an engine failure.

On *23 May 1969*, a Lockheed C130E Hercules registered 63-7789 (on the United States military aircraft register) was flown on an illegal flight by a inebriated United States Air Force crew chief, who took off early that morning. He flew the aircraft from RAF Mildenhall over the Thames estuary before turning towards Brighton with the intention of flying back to his home airbase in Virginia. Needless to say, he never made it. After flying out over the English Channel, he turned northwest, before turning again in a southerly direction north of Cherbourg, heading towards a point roughly twenty miles north of Alderney. However, by this point, two North American F-100 Super Sabres of the United States Air Force (a type of supersonic fighter jet used by the USAF until the late 1970s) were onto the aircraft and shot it down twenty miles to the north of Alderney. The aircraft plummeted into the sea and the pilot was killed immediately.

Sometime during *August 1980*, an Alderney Air Ferries Britten-Norman Islander, registered G-BEOC, crashed at Bournemouth when the pilot incorrectly calculated how much fuel would be required, resulting in the aircraft crash landing in a paddock, a few miles short of the airfield at Hurn. The reason for the incident was deemed to be human error. This was one of the events that ultimately led to AAF going bankrupt.

On *29 June 1995*, an Agusta Bell 206B Jet Ranger II helicopter registered G-BHXU was on a one-hour-and-fifty-minute flight from Liskeard in Cornwall to Deauville in France. The flight was uneventful until, close to Alderney, the pilot and engineer, the only two on board, experienced problems with yaw (turning unintentionally from side to side), accompanied by strange noises coming from the engine and transmission. At the same time, a warning light illuminated on the pilot's control panel. The pilot issued a mayday call and after two minutes the noise worsened, accompanied by further yaw problems and decay in engine power, leading him to ditch the helicopter in the sea. The descent was carried out slowly giving both occupants time to prepare and don lifejackets (the Air Accidents Investigation Branch accident report somewhat bizarrely states that this gave them time to remove their sunglasses). They both escaped alive and were rescued twenty-one minutes later at 15.30 by a Search and Rescue Sea King helicopter from RNAS Portland.

On *7 June 1997*, a Gardan Horizon GY80-150 aircraft, registered G-ATXF, was flying from Popham in Hampshire to Montelimar in France, routing via Jersey, for a fly-in for that type of aircraft. The aircraft was flying into headwinds at 2,000 feet over the English Channel and the pilot requested a diversion to Alderney to refuel. As he passed the lighthouse, Alderney Tower cleared the pilot for an approach onto Runway 26. Less than a minute after this, he declared a mayday because his engine was failing due to the lack of fuel. Tower cleared him to land on any runway; however, he advised them that he would have to ditch, and he did so near a fishing boat that collected him shortly afterwards. The aircraft was not recovered but the pilot survived with no injuries, albeit slightly shocked.

On *11 October 1997*, a Cessna F337F registered G-AZKO, was flying from Wellesbourne Mountford to Alderney with a pilot and two passengers on board. The flight was uneventful, and the pilot lowered the landing gear: three green lights were displayed in the cockpit, showing that the wheels were down and locked. As the pilot brought the aircraft down onto Runway 26, a warning horn sounded which he supposed was the stall warning horn, but actually the noise emitted was by the undercarriage horn, meaning that the wheels were retracted. The wheels collapsed as he landed, resulting in the aircraft sliding off the side of the runway onto the grass. In the subsequent investigation, the undercarriage, the indicator lights, and the microswitches triggering them, were all found to work correctly, leaving the cause of the collapse unexplained. Nobody was injured in the incident.

On *17 July 2001*, a Britten-Norman Trislander, registered G-BDTO of Aurigny, was flying in fog to Alderney from Guernsey. The pilot had decided to fly at a reduced speed to Alderney due to bad conditions there, giving them a chance to improve. There was a strong wind and standing water on the runway as well as bad visibility. Sure enough, though, the conditions did improve, and he approached the airfield using the NDB navigational aid. Having touched down, the pilot applied full braking and pushed forward on the control column. The aircraft continued to move and, despite his efforts to stop it, it exited the runway at about 20 mph. It then went through a light fence and crossed a public footpath before coming to a halt in a field after about 70 metres. It then stopped and two workmen nearby were able to assist passengers out of the aircraft. Those in row 3 were initially unable to exit because the door is protected by an interlock such that it cannot be opened while either of the magnetos fitted to the left engine is 'live'. The pilot made the magnetos 'safe' by turning them off and the aircraft was fully evacuated. No one was injured. The subsequent investigation showed that a gust of wind had blown the aircraft down the wet runway. This meant that with the aircraft aquaplaning over standing water patches, the pilot was unable to stop it, even with full braking applied. This may have been because of the pilot pushing forward on his control column, and subsequently shifting the weight from the main wheels, thereby reducing the effectiveness of the brakes.

On *25 September 2003*, a Beechcraft 58 Baron registered N23659 was being flown for the revalidation of a licence rating. Air traffic control at Alderney were told that the wheels would be lowered at a late stage in the approach. As the aircraft turned onto final approach, the commander selected the gear lever to the down position. The examiner told the commander that he could not see the three green down-and-locked lights, to which the pilot responded that this was normal as he had selected the lights to the 'dim' setting. The pilot then selected the lights to 'bright' and both men confirmed that they could see three greens. However, when the aircraft touched down, it became apparent that the wheels were still retracted. The aircraft slid off the runway, scraping its underside. The air traffic controller was expecting a late selection of the undercarriage so had no time to warn the pilot. Both occupants were uninjured, but the fire crew confirmed to the subsequent investigation team that the selector was in the down position. The result of the investigation was that in the act of switching the gear lights to 'bright', the pilot had inadvertently moved the switch to the 'Test' position, which resulted in three greens being shown. The gear warning horn had not sounded throughout the approach and because the pilot had put the lights to 'test', the 'gear unsafe' light may not have illuminated.

On *30 January 2004*, a Piper PA-34 Malibu Mirage registered G-BYLM was being flown onto Runway 26, the east-west runway, in a strong crosswind. The pilot had 3,900 hours, of which 700 were on the type, and he used a wing-down technique to cater for the wind. He touched down normally, but the aircraft then veered to the right, resulting in strong left rudder and braking being applied. The nose wheel then collapsed, resulting in the nose of the aircraft, and subsequently the propeller, contacting the runway. The aircraft came to rest about 200 yards up the runway. The Air Accidents Investigation Branch concluded that it was due to fractures and corrosion on the front wheel and undercarriage assembly that had not been seen due to non-compliance with the advice issued by the aircraft manufacturer to check on it every 100 hours of flying time.

A Piper PA-32R-300 Cherokee Lance, registered G-BTCA, after its crash in August 2009. Fire gutted the aircraft after its occupants had escaped to safety. (*James Varley*)

On *28 January 2008*, a Robin HR200 registered G-GBXF approached the airport normally and touched down. It was on a flight to refresh a Private Pilot's Licence, and there was an instructor and pilot onboard. Having touched down, the aircraft's right side dropped lower than the left and the wing contacted the ground, resulting in the aircraft twisting to the right and coming to rest on the grass. Later investigation showed that part of the undercarriage was already fractured and the resulting incident occurred because the slightly heavier than normal landing resulted in it separating completely. Both occupants were unhurt.

On the morning of *27 March 2008*, an EADS Socata TBM 700C1 registered N700GY landed at Alderney with three greens and one red displayed on the pilot's control panel. The pilot thought that this meant it was safe to land, but it was not because the red takes precedence over the three greens as it means that the wheels are down but not locked. As he touched down, the wheels collapsed and the aircraft rolled onto the grass. The pilot had not realised that he would have to lower the undercarriage using the emergency hand pump because the wording in the owner's manual had been so vague. It says that, 'One red warning light indicates that landing gears are operating, or not locked down or up.' Since this incident, the wording in the owner's manual has been amended.

On *26 March 2009*, a French lady who had flown into Alderney was taxiing to the grass parking area when her seat readjusted itself, resulting in her not being able to reach the rudder or brake pedals. This, in turn, meant that she could not steer the aircraft on the ground. It subsequently veered off the taxiway and through the boundary fence, before stopping with its propeller entangled in a heather bush.

On *23 August 2009*, a Piper PA-32R-300 Cherokee Lance aircraft crashed to the east of the airfield and a fire fighter who was sitting with his son nearby was able to help the occupants to safety. The aircraft caught fire soon afterwards and was badly damaged. The cause of the crash was that the pilot lost sight of the runway due to a bank of fog and the aircraft subsequently hit a thermal and stalled, crashing to the ground. The occupants escaped alive but slightly injured, one person injuring their leg. The aircraft was written off and deregistered in late 2009.

On *2 September 2009*, at approximately 5 o'clock in the afternoon, G-RLON, an Aurigny Trislander, was flying in from Southampton. When the pilot was informed of a 25-knot crosswind, outside of the aircraft's limits, he requested a go-around and permission to land on Alderney's grass Runway 14, facing more into the wind. As he was flying the aircraft over the threshold, a sharp and sudden downdraft and some turbulence caused the aircraft to make an early and unexpected landing, just before the beginning of the runway. After the pilot had shut down the engines, a passenger informed him that the aircraft had 'clipped' a marker board (showing the beginning of the grass runway) as he landed. This was confirmed by the fire service, who also noticed that two 70 cm (27 inch) fence posts had been dislodged and the fence wire clipped. The aircraft had landed 67 metres (220 feet) short of the runway threshold and minor damage was sustained to the right wheel support and housing.

Chapter 8
Channel Islands Air Search

Some of the proceeds of this book will go to Channel Islands Air Search. This worthy cause owes its origins to a group of pilots at Guernsey Airlines (taken over by Aurigny in 1988), most from boating backgrounds but some who had flown various aircraft from the Trislander to the Boeing 747. They were all too aware of the treacherous tidal flows and currents regularly experienced in the seas surrounding the Channel Islands, and seeing the value of an aircraft flying at low level for locating vessels and people in difficulty, they set up Guernsey Air Search as a part-time operation in 1980, using a Piper Aztec (registered G-BBWM) made available by Guernsey Airlines.

The local lifeboat crews and later the States of Guernsey soon saw the value of such a facility and a charitable trust was soon set up to purchase and operate the Aztec. The generosity of the Lions Club of Guernsey financed the purchase of this aircraft, hence its name, *Lions Pride*. As the service covered the entire Channel Islands area, including French coastal waters, it was later renamed Channel Islands Air Search (CIAS). The trustees then faced the task of raising the necessary funds to operate the aircraft since the charity is not in any way subsidised by the States and is entirely independent. Fundraising has been undertaken throughout the Channel Islands and the generosity of people and businesses has ensured that CIAS has been able to maintain and operate its aircraft.

By the early 1990s, an upgrade was needed, so in 1992 a Britten-Norman Islander was purchased specifically for the task. Again, the Lions Clubs in both Jersey and Guernsey made major contributions to the fundraising for the purchase. Modifications would need to be carried out to give the aircraft the correct equipment, and these were also funded by the Lions Clubs, Friends of Air Search and also the public. Nineteen non-standard modifications were carried out in the space of one year, all approved by the CAA, which included adding an extended nose that housed marine radar.

The Islander soon carried a unique range of equipment – most of which is sourced from marine origin due to a lower cost than aviation-specific items – such as a chute in the floor to drop strobe lights or smoke generators; an onboard computer for the Search Directors; marine GPS and radar; and also FLIR (Forward Looking Infra Red). This is especially useful in bad visibility or during the hours of darkness, but it was not until 2000 that one was developed that was small enough to fit in the Islander. This sits in a

CHANNEL ISLANDS
AIRSEARCH
The Lifeboats' Eyes in the Sky

Some of the proceeds from this book will go to Channel Islands Air Search, a charity that helps to save lives at sea.

football sized sphere under the radome and can, together with a video camera, produce a clear picture in total darkness. There is a loud hailer to reassure divers and those who have no radios that the boats are coming to assist, and also an air-launchable dinghy which can accommodate up to eleven people. The most recent addition to the Islander's inventory is a Traffic Avoidance System, fitted in early 2010. This is especially useful when operating in close proximity with other search aircraft (especially helicopters) in giving their exact location. However, the crew all agree that the most important asset is the human eyeball.

The year 1995 saw the next major project undertaken, which was the construction of a purpose-built hangar at Guernsey Airport to house the aircraft and crew facilities. This is especially important as it protects the aircraft from the worst of the saline air, which can induce corrosion.

CIAS continues to flourish – in 2005, the team won the Queen's Award for Voluntary Service, and they continue to be the lifeboats' eyes in the skies to this day. The organisation also continues to help both British and French lifeboats, as well as search-and-rescue helicopters from both countries, thereby saving time and money as well as lives – and all with a call-out time of only thirty minutes.

CIAS' broad remit includes searching for lost or stricken pleasure boats, fishing boats, wind surfers, ditched aircraft, divers, people who have fallen overboard from ferries, and also encompasses coastal searches for people missing on shore. However, not all searches end in success.

Many searches are long and drawn-out and therefore immensely uncomfortable – particularly bad are those at cliff height or below. Some people think that Trislander flights are turbulent but they, according to the crew at CIAS, have seen nothing as flights on the Islander are usually twice as bumpy, challenging even the strongest of stomachs.

Channel Islands Air Search saves the time and money of the RNLI Lifeboats, but more importantly the lives of stricken sailors and people. Notable successes include a yachtsman whose boat had sunk – he was located within ten minutes of takeoff – and also several incidents where divers had become separated from their support vessels, including three near Sark who were located within fifteen minutes of takeoff, and another near Alderney where CIAS directed a nearby Condor ferry to the casualty.

By buying this book, you are supporting the Lifeboats' eyes in the sky who, with further publicity but more importantly financial support, can continue to save the lives of stricken Channel Islanders in times of great need. It should be remembered that CIAS depends entirely on public generosity with little support from the States. The organisation therefore needs all the help it can get to continue its crucial work into the future.

Incidentally, when the Islander came into service, G-BBWM was decommissioned and stripped out. The empty aircraft was then shipped to London, where it was suspended from the roof of the exhibition hall that was holding the Boat Show; it formed the centrepiece of the Guernsey Tourism stand. When the exhibition was over, the aircraft was returned to Alderney where it was positioned on the fire training ground at the airport, painted grey and used as their training aircraft. It remains there to this day.

The author is indebted for inexhaustible information regarding Channel Islands Air Search to Ian Larby, Honorary Secretary to the charity.

Chapter 9
The Flying Squad – Island Aviators of Today

SALLY BARBER: *FORMER AURIGNY PILOT*

An Aurigny pilot for nineteen years, Sally Barber has spent most of her life in aviation. Both her father and cousin were RAF pilots (with the former serving in the Second World War), and she has enjoyed aviation from an early age, moving from one RAF station to another fairly frequently, depending on where her father was stationed.

Sally gained her Pilot's License at the age of twenty-two and went on to be a stewardess with British Airways. Having spent some years doing this, Sally went on to pilot for Guernsey Airlines, flying their Shorts 330s on routes across the UK. When the airline was bought by Aurigny, she moved to Jersey European, being stationed for six months in Belfast as well as several other locations throughout the country, again flying on regional routes around the British Isles.

Sally soon returned to the Channel Islands, however, to become Aurigny's first female pilot. By now, she had a good deal of experience on the Shorts 330 and 360 series so it seemed silly not to take her on. She ended up flying these, together with Aurigny's new Saab 340s, which were particularly enjoyed among flight crew because they were more modern aircraft than the older Shorts. However, her heart really lay in flying the Trislanders, especially to and from Alderney. The community spirit, in Sally's opinion, is unbeatable and you get to know the regular passengers as well as those who make use of the air ambulance service. At the same time as having 100 per cent faith in these trusty aircraft, Sally has had some interesting experiences.

On one occasion, the Trislander she was flying was struck by lightning. While being entirely harmless to all on board due to the aircraft not being earthed, the strike did make a small hole in both the nose and the tail of the aircraft, where it entered and exited. Sally also once experienced an engine failure while leaving Southampton – two cylinders on the rear engine failed, resulting in the back of the aircraft being covered in oil. Although this may sound dramatic, it should be noted that the Trislander has an impeccable safety record without a single fatality in Aurigny's history, spanning over four decades – no mean feat for an airline.

Sally stopped flying for Aurigny on her birthday in July 2009 due to a restriction on the age of single crew meaning that only those under sixty may fly. She is now a jurat in the Alderney court and in her spare time is also a member of the St John's Ambulance team.

Sally Barber flew for Aurigny for over 19 years and has spent most of her life in aviation.

Ralph Burridge: *Aurigny Pilot and former Chief Flying Instructor of both the Alderney & Guernsey Flying Clubs.*

Educated at Pinner County Grammar School, Ralph Burridge spent a good deal of his pre-Alderney life in Middlesex. He fulfilled his childhood ambition to 'play with real aeroplanes' when in 1955 he was offered an apprenticeship at the Handley Page Company at Cricklewood in London.

He soon became a draughtsman in the design office, working on the Victor bomber. Soon he had risen to a position in the company's Technical Publications department, staying there until the company ceased to exist in the early 1960s. It was while working for HP that he came into contact with real flying when he joined the Handley Page Gliding Club. However, gliding for Burridge was a five-minute wonder, for as soon as he had flown as a passenger in the Auster glider tug, his determination to fly 'real aeroplanes' was established.

Ralph Burridge also flew for Aurigny and is former Chief Flying Instructor for both Alderney and Guernsey Flying Clubs.

The year 1962 saw Ralph join a firm of engineering equipment suppliers. While not being a job he particularly enjoyed, it did mean that as director of the holding company and managing director of a subsidiary, he was able to finance the flying and attain his first instructing qualification. After leaving the company in 1971, he formed a four-branch travel company, which he sold so as to be able to move to Alderney in 1974.

As a qualified instructor, Ralph was to spend a good deal of time in Guernsey instructing for both Channel Aviation and the Guernsey Aero Club, as well as undertaking air taxi work for Astra Aviation. In 1979, he joined Aurigny Air Services, during which time he became their Chief Training Captain. It was at this time that he was appointed to the UK Panel of Examiners, the body responsible to the CAA for monitoring the overall standards of pilot training and the quality of flying instructing.

At the age of sixty, as with all aircraft flying commercially and operated as 'single crew', legislation meant that he could no longer carry passengers. However, although having to retire from that role in 1998, he was still able to carry out all forms of pilot training, together with flight testing of company pilots; so he remained with Aurigny as a Training Captain until his second 'retirement' in 2003. As an instructor, he is still permitted to train aircrew, an arrangement which, although it could continue indefinitely, is likely to come to an end in 2011, when he is seriously considering retiring for the third and final time.

Burridge does have some funny recollections as a pilot for Aurigny – on one occasion, the entire compliment of passenger were not English-speaking and as a result must have completely misunderstood the safety briefing. Presumably assuming that as the Safety Card was being shown to them for a good reason, they decided to take the picture instructions literally, pulling out the lifejackets from under the seats, donning them and then inflating them.

Another rather amusing occasion was when it seemed that there was a possible problem with the nose wheel steering on the Trislander freighter flight that Ralph was flying: what it would do on landing was uncertain. In the event, all was well and nothing happened, but having seen firsthand the mess that had been made inside a car when his wife had collided with a lamppost with several bowls of rice pudding on the passenger seat, he did not fancy the same outcome – the aircraft was carrying a full load of yoghurt, and the cartoon image in his mind of appearing from the aircraft, covered from head to foot with yoghurt, looking like some alien life form, stayed with him for some time afterwards.

Ralph hopes to see private aviation continue on Alderney into the future – however he, together with many others, realises that the rise in the price of fuel will have a huge impact. He now lives with his wife near the airport – close enough that when he does finally retire, he will still see and hear the aircraft he used to fly.

Richard Herivel: *Private Pilot*

Richard Herivel can trace his Alderney family back to 1647 – he was born and bred on the island and has had a long association with aviation. Obtaining his Pilot's Licence at just twenty-one years old, he went on to own several aircraft, including an American-built Luscombe, dating from 1946, and later a Murphy Rebel, which came in kit form – he subsequently spent seven years building it after its delivery on 31 August 1997.

He had only ever wanted to be a private pilot as his real interest lies in engineering, having trained as a fitter 'on the job' at a Bournemouth-based company. He worked for Aurigny's operations department, and later worked for Stratair Engineering in Alderney as well as Air Sarnia Line Maintenance.

Herivel now uses his Murphy Rebel – which he entirely coincidentally painted in Aurigny's second colour scheme – as an airborne car to do his shopping and visit friends in Guernsey and Cherbourg. Most trips are quite mundane, which he sees as a good thing. The fogs and hazes of June and July can be a challenge, but generally he finds Alderney a wonderful place to fly.

As well as its day-to-day island-hopping duties, the Rebel has been flown all over western Europe by Herivel, accompanied by friends and family. He is now a carpenter, but still has a passion for aircraft, including remote control miniatures, which he flies on his farm and around the island.

Coming from a long-established Alderney family, Richard Herivel has his own kit-built aircraft, which he flies regularly to Guernsey and elsewhere.

Keith Webster took the joint role of Airport Manager and Breakwater Superintendent in late 1987. Since then, his role has grown to include looking after the States of Alderney's computer network.

KEITH WEBSTER: *AIRPORT MANAGER*

Having had a long association with aviation in Alderney, Keith Webster finally became Airport Manager on 28 September 1987. His father was Leader of the Fire Service, retiring in 1981, and he was born on the island. Having been educated in Guernsey, he left school in 1969 to join the Board of Trade the following year.

Having trained in electronics, and more specifically air traffic engineering, he was posted near Heathrow with a company specialising in radio navigational beacons. It was quite normal for him to travel all over the UK repairing the beacons, and he would sometimes relieve the engineer at Britain's only manned beacon at Alderney – this was because it was so hard to get engineers to the island when the beacon developed a fault.

Soon, he had found his way to management, but was becoming increasingly impatient with the ever lengthening commute between his home at Sandhurst and Heathrow. He spotted a vacancy for a job with multiple roles in Alderney – this incorporated the job of Airport Manager, a new position, with that of Breakwater Superintendent.

The job took on a different identity in 1998 when Keith was put in charge of the States of Alderney's computer system as well as his previous two jobs – when he joined, there had been about ten standalone computers, but he linked these together so that now sixty computers sit on a central network, using email servers in Guernsey. Now a three-part job, it is a little more challenging but Webster still finds time to be President of the Alderney Football Association, ever hopeful of another victory.

Keith believes that the future of the airfield mainly depends on the population – it would have to more than double to warrant expansion to take larger aircraft. If it contracted, then services would be reduced to a shuttle service to Guernsey with connections around Britain.

Chapter 10
The Future

Alderney airport's facilities have been questioned numerous times in the last decade but various problems – such as the absence of refuelling for aircraft in 2005, due to lack of storage space – have been resolved. Another problem for the airport has been the CAA's increasingly tight regulations on security, customs, and health and safety. As a result of these, numerous portacabins have had to be used to satisfy the regulations, making the airport rather untidy – it could be argued that it now resembles a caravan park more than the airport it used to be.

There have been calls, therefore, to put the contents of these new portacabins inside in a new building. A new structure would also alleviate the problems experienced with the felted flat roof of the terminal, which is liable to leak quite easily. Many tourists who visit the island enjoy the quaint and old-fashioned feeling it retains, lost long ago by most English communities. However, for some islanders the novelty has rather worn off and forty people waiting to board a plane on a fogbound autumn morning is not always the definition of fun that immediately springs to mind.

A good example of the sort of building needed is at Connemara Airport on the west coast of Ireland, around thirty miles from Galway. Serving the very small Aran Islands using 8-seater Britten-Norman Islanders, the airport has a 600 metre bitumen runway and a cosy but modern terminal that does the job very well, costing little in the way of maintenance.

However, opponents of a new terminal in Alderney say that it would not be worth it for an island that receives relatively few tourists and has a comparatively small population – it would therefore be a waste of public money to carry out such improvements, as well as a shame to spoil the quaint feeling retained by the basic (yet arguably adequate) airport facilities. While expansion may be an attractive opportunity, it would also be a huge drain on States' money: to carry out a project that may not greatly benefit the island and might cost a lot public money would be foolhardy.

In 2006, the States of Guernsey commissioned Burks Green, a consultancy firm from Nottinghamshire, to formulate a master plan for the future of Alderney airport. The plan showed that extending (but more probably, entirely rebuilding) the runway would be necessary to accommodate any larger sorts of aircraft, namely the de Havilland Dash 8-100 or the Dornier 328 – both aircraft that seat around thirty-five passengers. However, the use of these aircraft would require the rebuilding of the runway and taxiway structures and also an upgrade in terminal facilities to accommodate the predicted rise in passenger numbers. Aircraft parking facilities would also have to be upgraded to give more space, probably by turning some of the present grass parking area for light aircraft into a tarmac area for the new and larger types of passenger aircraft.

If the runway were to be extended to accommodate these aircraft types, it would probably have another 200 metres (650 feet) added to the west. That said, Aurigny have confirmed during meetings with the Airport Manager, Keith Webster, that they can probably keep their Trislanders airworthy as long as aviation fuel is easily available. As well as this, a similar study on Guernsey airport in a Billet d'État showed that smaller aircraft with a higher frequency of flights would be more beneficial than larger aircraft with lower frequency. This applies to Alderney because Trislanders are not often full, so it would therefore be uneconomical to fly larger aircraft into the island; and if they were, it would have to be on far more irregular services. However, at peak times such as Alderney Week, a distinct weakness emerges – as Aurigny have only five operational Trislanders at any one time, of which at least two must be deployed on their other inter-island and French routes, three Trislanders cannot provide a service that caters for the demand from Southampton and Guernsey, as it is a regular occurrence for all flights to be full for three days before large island events.

Parts are not a problem for the Trislanders, however, as engines are readily available – there is a plentiful second-hand supply, and Lycoming, the firm who manufactured the engines, are still offering support. Wings can be obtained from Britten-Norman Defenders (the military variant of the Islander that first flew in 1971) and require minimum modification. Aviation fuel, meanwhile, could still be around for another thirty-five years, albeit at a higher cost. Therefore, bearing in mind that the Trislanders were built around the 1970s, they could theoretically be up to seventy years old by the time they are retired. However, airlines serving the Channel Islands will probably have more economical solutions by that time.

If the Trislanders were, for some reason, to become entirely uneconomical or impossible to keep airworthy, then the replacement would probably be the Twin Otter, a nineteen-seat, versatile aircraft that was used in Alderney in the 1980s in a trial by Aurigny that proved unsuccessful due to the reduction in engine life caused by the high number of starts and short flight times that are associated with inter-island flying. This problem has now been solved, and the aircraft is back in production. The Twin Otter would probably be the most favourable option due to the fire service capabilities not having to be altered and the runway not having to be lengthened. Another alternative is a new design by a French company named GECI International. The aircraft, called the Skylander, was partly designed under the supervision of the late Desmond Norman (of Britten-Norman), and is projected, at the time of writing, to have its maiden flight in 2011 – a mock-up of the fuselage was displayed at the 2009 airshow at Le Bourget in Paris. It can be configured to take nineteen passengers, or to carry between four and sixteen passengers in a combined passenger/cargo configuration.

Other alternatives that would mean the airport would have to make minor alterations include the Dornier 228, the Fairchild Metro and the BAe Jetstream 31, a British aircraft already used by Blue Islands, also with nineteen seats, as well as the LET 410, another nineteen-seat aircraft, being the most popular small turboprop in history with over

Alderney's control tower. The cabin mounted at the top of the stilts replaced a more basic wooden structure in 1988. (*Ian Haskell*)

1,000 built. It has not found acceptance with many regional airlines in the west; built in Czechoslovakia during Soviet rule, it could be argued that the aircraft's safety record leaves a little to be desired.

However, Britten-Norman is still accepting orders for the Trislander and it would have restarted production in the late 1990s due to China Northern Airlines placing an order, but the airline went bankrupt before production began. Britten-Norman has previously disclosed that the Trislander production line would be restarted, but the notice on its website was later changed to say that it was offering refurbishment and it would consider new-build aircraft.

Twin Otters are now being manufactured once more in Canada by a firm named Viking Air, which offers it in seaplane configuration or for land-based airports. They are also much more modern and comfortable for pilot and passenger alike than previous versions of the aircraft. They can still, however, take off and land on a postage stamp (according to many an air instructor) so would be ideal for the island.

At the time of writing, Aurigny is also in talks with the CAA about developing a Global Positioning System (GPS) approach pattern into Alderney. Depending on the system installed, it could result in aircraft being able to make an approach to land in less visibility. This might result in fewer of the delays that are regularly experienced due to the fog in the Islands. However, as all such systems must be tested biannually, this would be expensive as a CAA aircraft would have to be sent to the island to conduct the tests, which would apparently be more in-depth than those conducted on the NDB.

In an age where comfortable jet travel most definitely leads the way, Trislanders have a mixed reputation with pilots and passengers alike. One traveller posted a video onto an internet video-sharing website showing water dripping through the window onto his seat while in flight. Trislanders are generally only remembered, by those mainlanders who have visited the Channel Islands, for giving some of the most hair-raising and bumpy (but also exciting) flights they will ever have. Having served Channel Islanders well for the past forty years, might they not do so for another forty?

Technical Information

Radio Frequencies (all in MHz unless otherwise stated):

- Alderney Tower: 125.35
- Alderney Approach (only used in Air Races or Fly-Ins): 119.40, 124.50.
- Alderney Ground (only used in Air Races or Fly-Ins): 130.50
- Alderney Fire: 121.60
- NDB (ALD): 383 KHz

Guernsey Approach provides approach services to Alderney all year, using Guernsey Approach which operates on 128.65. The only exception to this is during the Air Races and formerly the Fly-in periods, when the airfield is extremely busy. During these times, Alderney Approach will be used and administered by a controller in Guernsey, simply to lighten the load on the Guernsey Approach frequency. Also at peak times, Alderney Ground will be used to direct those aircraft taxiing to park or take-off. Outside this period, 125.35 alone is used for both purposes. Channel Islands airspace is administered by Jersey Zone on 125.20.

Codes and Airport Information:

- ICAO: EGJA
- IATA: ACI
- Elevation (ASL): circa +280 feet – airfield is on a slight slope.

Runways, Lengths and Lighting:

- 08/26. Asphalt (partially grass) – 880 metres, lit.
- 03/21. Grass – 497 metres, not lit, closed to night operations.
- 32/14. Grass – 732 metres, lit with portable low-intensity lights.

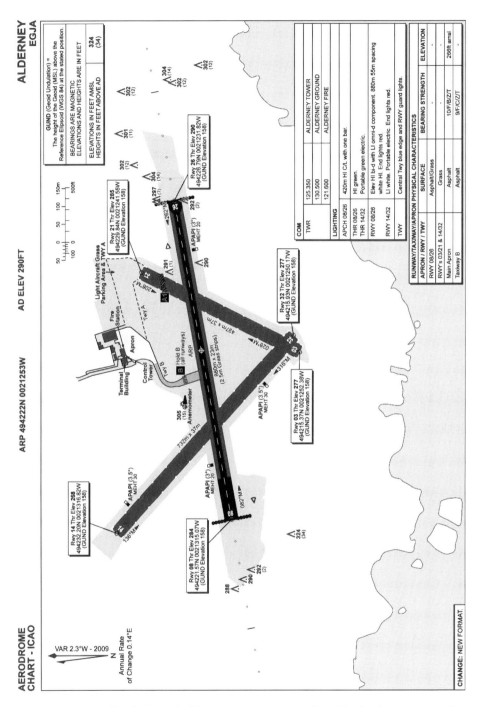

The current official chart of Alderney Airport. (*Reproduced by kind permission of the CAA – copyright Civil Aviation Authority*)

Glossary of Acronyms

- AAF: Alderney Air Ferries. An airline that operated in Alderney in the late 1970s to the early 1980s using Britten-Norman Islanders.
- ADF: Automatic Direction Finder. Instrument on an aircraft, which in conjunction with radio navigational aid can help a pilot gauge their location.
- AAIB: Air Accidents Investigation Branch. British governmental organisation for the investigation of aircraft accidents. They also investigate Channel Islands incidents.
- ASL: Above Sea Level. Measure for altimeters, the altitude-measuring instruments in aircraft, which can then be reset when they approach the airport to a measure of height above land, so that it shows zero when the aircraft touches the runway.
- BAe: British Aerospace. Now BAE Systems – constructed aircraft and parts from around 1970 to 2000. It built the last British civil jet aircraft, the 90-seater Avro RJ regional jet.
- BEA: British European Airways. It operated through Britain and Europe from the 1950s to the 1970s.
- BN: Britten-Norman. An aircraft company based on the Isle of Wight that built the Trislanders and now constructs the Islander and Defender aircraft. Sometimes also referred to as Pilatus Britten Norman (PBN) or Fairey Britten Norman (FBN) due to both companies owning BN at one time.
- BIA: British Island Airways. British airline that was based in the Channel Islands and Gatwick. It operated from the 1960s to the 1970s but did not run services to Alderney.
- BUA: British United Airways. Operated in Britain from the 1950s to the 1970s. British United Island Airways (BUIA) was their Channel Islands division.
- CAA: Civil Aviation Authority. British regulator for civil aviation.
- CIAS: Channel Islands Air Search. Airborne search and rescue charity based in Guernsey and equipped with a Britten-Norman Islander.
- DfT: Department for Transport. British governmental organisation in charge of the transport network, including air, sea, road and rail travel.
- DME: Distance Measuring Equipment. A navigational aid that displays to the pilot the distance from the source of transmission.

- G-XXXX: A British registration, G- being the British prefix and the other four letters identifying the individual aircraft.
- GPS: Global Positioning System. Uses satellite signal to determine location anywhere in the world.
- Hz, MHz and KHz: A measure of frequency, and in this context, radio frequency. The VHF Civil Aviation Band exists between 108 to 136 MHz.
- NDB: Non-Directional Beacon. Basic navigational aid.
- RAF: Royal Air Force. The British military force in the air.
- SAR: Search and Rescue. Operations carried out by any organisation helping those lost or stranded.
- SOE: Special Operations Executive. An organisation formed by Winston Churchill to conduct the war through methods other than direct military engagement, e.g. espionage.
- STOL: Short Take Off and Landing. Aircraft in this category are those with very short runway requirements. Most commercial aircraft that come to Alderney fit into this category.
- VHF: Very High Frequency. A band of radio frequency commonly used in aviation today. The VHF Civil Aviation Band extends from 108 to 136 MHz.
- VOR: Very High Frequency Omni Directional Range. Navigational aid for pilots to gauge their location, more complex than an NDB.

Index